EQUALITY OF OPPORTUNITY

EQUALITY
of
OPPORTUNITY

John E. Roemer

Harvard University Press
Cambridge, Massachusetts
London, England · 1998

Library of Congress Cataloging-in-Publication Data

Roemer, John E.
    Equality of opportunity / John E. Roemer.
        p.   cm.
    Includes bibliographical references and index.
    ISBN 0-674-25991-2 (alk. paper)
    1. Welfare economics—Mathematical models.   2. Distributive
justice—Mathematical models.   3. Equality—Mathematical models.
4. Competition—Mathematical models.   5. Social policy—Mathematical
models.   I. Title.
HB846.R63   1998
330.12'6—dc21   97-33525

Contents

Preface

I am indebted to Steven Durlauf, Ignacio Ortuño-Ortin, James Robinson, William Simon, and Peter Vallentyne, who each read parts of this manuscript and provided me with useful comments. My ideas have also been influenced by the contributors to a symposium, organized by Joshua Cohen and published in the *Boston Review* in 1995, in which Richard Epstein, Elizabeth Fox-Genovese, Susan Hurley, Eric Maskin, Arthur Ripstein, Nancy Rosenblum, Thomas Scanlon, Samuel Scheffler, and Robert Solow examined and critiqued an early version of my proposal. I have had useful discussions on parts of the manuscript with my colleague Joaquim Silvestre. Finally, as is so often the case, I am deeply indebted to G. A. Cohen, who read the manuscript and discussed its problems with me over an extended period. I am also grateful to participants at many seminars and conferences over the last several years who have commented on these ideas.

This essay oscillates, methodologically, between the philosophical and the economic. Within each method, I am confident that the technique is sufficiently elementary that the arguments can be understood by graduate students. Unfortunately, too few graduate students today who work in political philosophy or welfare economics have an understanding of both methods. I think that to do good political philosophy or welfare economics, it is essential to be cognizant of the main issues and ideas in both disciplines, if not to have both sets of technique in one's tool kit. Political philosophers with too little knowledge of welfare economics frequently try to reinvent the wheel, usually with bad results. Welfare economists who are poorly read in political philosophy often waste their time on technical questions that philosophy shows have no interest for the study of human welfare.

If this essay can at least illustrate the value of an interdisciplinary approach, it will have served one useful purpose.

July 1997

Yo soy: yo y mi circunstancia.

—José Ortega y Gasset

§1

Introduction

Two conceptions of equality of opportunity are prevalent today in Western democracies. The first says that society should do what it can to "level the playing field" among individuals who compete for positions, or, more generally, that it level the playing field among individuals during their periods of formation, so that all those with relevant potential will eventually be admissible to pools of candidates competing for positions. The second conception, which I call the nondiscrimination principle, states that, in the competition for positions in society, all individuals who possess the attributes relevant for the performance of the duties of the position in question be included in the pool of eligible candidates, and that an individual's possible occupancy of the position be judged only with respect to those relevant attributes. An instance of the first principle is that compensatory education be provided for children from disadvantaged social backgrounds, so that a larger proportion of them will acquire skills required to compete, later on, for jobs against persons with more advantaged childhoods. An instance of the second principle is that race or sex, as such, should not count for or against a person's eligibility for a position, when race or sex is an irrelevant attribute insofar as the performance of the duties of the position is concerned.

Indeed, one can view the nondiscrimination principle as deriving from a particular interpretation of the level-the-playing-field principle. That interpretation says that, in the presence of discrimination, some persons have an unfair advantage over others in the competition for positions, because their eligibility for the position in question is considered superior on account of social attitudes and practices which, indeed, should not count. The playing field is leveled by insisting that such attitudes and practice indeed *not* count.

1

But the typical application of the level-the-playing-field principle goes farther than the nondiscrimination principle. It might, for example, say that equal opportunity requires that educational expenditures per pupil in public schools be equalized in a state or country. Were such equalization not to have been implemented, then nondiscrimination alone, in the competition for jobs, would not constitute the provision of equal opportunity, for earlier the playing field was not leveled, if children from rich school districts had access to better education than did children from poor school districts. Indeed, equalizing per pupil expenditures may not go far enough toward leveling the playing field in such cases. If an educated child is the output forthcoming from applying a certain technology to a bundle of inputs or resources, some of which are "internal" to the child—his genes, his family, his neighborhood—and some of which can be supplied "externally" by the school district—teachers, schools, books—then leveling the playing field might be thought to require compensating those with inferior bundles of internal resources with an extra dose of external resources.

Among the citizens of any advanced democracy, we find individuals who hold a spectrum of views with respect to what is required for equal opportunity, from the nondiscrimination view at one pole to pervasive social provision to correct for all manner of disadvantage at the other. Common to all these views, however, is the precept that the equal-opportunity principle, at some point, holds the individual accountable for the achievement of the advantage in question, whether that advantage be a level of educational achievement, health, employment status, income, or the economist's utility or welfare. Thus there is, in the notion of equality of opportunity, a "before" and an "after": before the competition starts, opportunities must be equalized, by social intervention if need be, but after it begins, individuals are on their own. The different views of equal opportunity can be categorized according to where they place the starting gate which separates "before" from "after."

I attempt in this essay to propose a precise way that we can organize our disparate views about equal opportunity. More specifically, different people have different conceptions about where the starting gate should be, or about the degrees to which individuals should be held accountable for the outcomes or advantage they eventually enjoy. My purpose is to propose an algorithm which will enable a society (or a social planner) to translate any such view about personal accountability into a social policy that will implement a kind or degree of equal opportunity consonant with that view. If my algorithm is generally accepted as a reasonable one, then the political debate over what equality of opportunity requires can be reduced from one over social policy to a more fundamental debate about the proper realm of individual accountability. For once that realm has been agreed upon, or once a view of what that realm should be has been victorious through political competition, then a specific equal-opportunity policy will follow automatically, as it were, from the application of my proposed algorithm.

This should be contrasted to the way debate over equal opportunity takes place today, which is primarily over what the social policy should be. But that debate is often confused, as the participants do not share a common notion or definition of what equality of opportunity consists in. I propose, if you will, a definition of equal opportunity. It will not resolve the debate, but it can force it to take place over questions which are more fundamental than the choice of one particular social policy or another.

I have just said that my aim is pluralistic, in the sense that I shall provide a tool that can be used to calculate an equal-opportunity policy consonant with any of a spectrum of views of individual accountability. It is pluralistic in another sense as well. People with many different conceptions of what distributive justice consists in endorse equality of opportunity. I do not intend to advocate a particular conception of distributive justice, or even the view that distributive justice consists in some form of equal opportunity. (Perhaps I believe that to be the case, but it is a case I shall not prosecute here.) People who hold various theories of distributive justice advocate the provision of equal opportunity not only in different degrees (that is, with different conceptions of accountability) but also in different spheres of social life. I shall endeavor to respect this variety of views by showing how the algorithm of equal opportunity that I propose can be applied in specific spheres. Sections 8, 9, and 10 will apply the algorithm to the spheres of health, education, and employment, and section 11 presents a summary of an attempt to calculate the educational policy that would equalize opportunities for earning income in the United States. It is my hope, then, that persons from many points on the political spectrum will be able to use my proposal without committing themselves to a more pervasive egalitarianism than they are prepared to endorse.

I use two techniques in this essay, the philosophic and the economic. The former is used to locate the relevant concepts and to put forth a definition of equality of opportunity (principally in sections 2, 3, and to some extent in sections 12 and 14); the latter is used to move from the conceptual and somewhat imprecise level to a precise definition and consequent social policy. The preponderance of "economic" sections is due not to my thinking that the philosophical aspects of the problem are easier or fewer but, rather, to my being a trained economist and an untrained philosopher. Consequently, my economic imagination is considerably more developed than my philosophical one, a personal misfortune reflected in the sectional distribution of techniques. That having been said, I wish to emphasize that this essay's immediate intellectual forebears are the writings of three philosophers: Ronald Dworkin (1981a, 1981b), Richard Arneson (1989, 1990), and G. A. Cohen (1989). Although in the interest of brevity I do not attempt here to explain how my views descend from theirs, I have tried to do so in a recent book (Roemer 1996, chaps. 7, 8).

As the nondiscrimination principle is well known, this essay's task is to articulate carefully the "level-playing-field" view of equal opportunity. I will usually identify equality of opportunity with its "level-the-playing-field" interpretation. It is only in sections 12 and 14 that the nondiscrimination view is specifically discussed, and contrasted with the more inclusive level-the-playing-field view. It is in section 12 that I propose how we may decide what the scope of each of these two principles should be on the domain of social allocation issues.

Circumstances, Types, and Autonomous Choice

I shall assume, then, that the purpose of an equal-opportunity policy is to level the playing field. What features, in the backgrounds of the individuals in question, correspond to the mounds and troughs in the playing field that should be leveled off? I propose that these are the differential circumstances of individuals for which we believe they should not be held accountable, and which affect their ability to achieve or have access to the kind of advantage that is being sought. To be concrete, consider the access to a good life that is facilitated or made possible by education. Our society considers education a sufficiently important input into the good life that it views the social provision of a decent education to all individuals as necessary for equalizing opportunities for attaining the good life. Indeed, providing equal opportunities might seem to require providing equal amounts of educational resources for all individuals, and this goal has been achieved to varying extents in different countries and states. In the United States, education has historically been funded by municipalities, and this engenders unequal schools for municipalities with unequal tax bases or for municipalities which decide to fund education at different levels. A number of states have attempted to equalize educational resources by cutting the link between local taxes and school funding. In California, for instance, there is a law requiring the state to fund local public schools so that an equal amount is spent on each student in the state. The landmark *Brown* case (1954) provided that equal education for blacks and whites required that schools be integrated: the previous "separate but equal" policy was, it was ruled, oxymoronic. But in the United States, even were public educational financing to be equalized per capita, educational funding would not be equalized, because of the existence of private schools. In the Nordic countries, private schooling is for all practical purposes unavailable.

Guaranteeing equal per capita financing of educational facilities is, however, not sufficient to provide equal educational achievement, since different children are able to use educational resources (teachers, books, school buildings) with different degrees of effectiveness or efficiency. To take an extreme case, mentally retarded children will require more resources than normal children to reach a similar level of functioning, or at least a level that we find to be acceptable. That we provide more educational resources for such children shows that we do not think that equal opportunity for the good life, insofar as the educational dimension is relevant, is achieved by providing equal educational resources per capita: we believe that more resources should be provided to some types of child if those children are unable to process the resources as effectively as others. The problem is to decide: when is it the case that different types of child are unable to process resources with equal effectiveness, and when is it the case that, though able to process them equally effectively, they do not by virtue of choice?

We must distinguish between the circumstances beyond a child's control which influence her ability to process educational resources and her acts of autonomous volition and effort. Equalizing opportunity for the good life, insofar as education is an input—or, more precisely, equalizing opportunity for educational achievement—requires distributing educational resources in such a way that the differential abilities of children to turn resources into educational achievement are compensated for, where those abilities are determined by circumstances beyond the control of the individual. Differential achievements due to the application of autonomous volition, however, should not be "leveled" or compensated for by an equal-opportunity policy.

Thus I am defining the "ability" of a child to transform resources into educational achievement as the propensity she has to effect that transformation, by virtue of the influence of circumstances beyond her control, which—let us say, for the moment—include her genes, her family background, her culture, and more generally, her social milieu, to the extent that that milieu is unchosen. But two children with the same relevant circumstances, and hence the same ability, may achieve different amounts of education by virtue of applying different amounts of effort. One extreme possibility is that circumstances determine everything, so that there is no room left for autonomous effort: if this were true, then we would say that what appears to be differential effort is in fact fully determined by circumstances beyond the control of the individuals. This case, which I call the deterministic case, is just one possibility. The general case is that educational achievement is determined jointly by circumstances and freely chosen effort, and equality of opportunity requires compensating persons for the differences in their circumstances, insofar as those differences affect educational achievement, but not compensating them for the consequences of the differential application of effort.

Suppose—a tall order—that we knew exactly what circumstances jointly determined a child's ability to process resources into educational achievement. Suppose, further, the circumstances of a child could be precisely characterized as the value of a certain vector with, say, n components. Let us suppose, for simplicity, that this vector takes on a number of values in the population, considerably fewer than the number of individuals. Then we could partition the population of children in question into a set of *types*, where a type consists of all individuals whose value of this vector is the same. (In practice, we would define a type as the set of persons whose circumstantial vectors were almost the same.) By definition of ability and type, all individuals in a given type have the same ability to transform resources into educational achievement. By supposition, there are, on average, a fairly large number of individuals in the average type, since the number of types is small compared with the number of individuals. Let us further suppose that there is a large number of individuals in each type.

I would construct the equal-opportunity policy as follows. Suppose we distribute the educational resources in a way so that, within each type, each individual receives the same amount of resources. (There may be, however, different per capita amounts of the resource for different types.) We will observe, in all likelihood, a *distribution* of effort levels in each type, leading to differential educational achievements within each type. (I am here assuming that effort is one-dimensional and measurable.) Note that this distribution is itself a characteristic of the type, not of any individual. *Where* on that distribution an individual sits is, however, by construction, due to his choice of effort.

I propose that the equal-opportunity policy must equalize, in some average sense yet to be defined, the educational achievements of all types, but not equalize the achievements within types, which differ according to effort. Thus equality of opportunity requires compensating individuals with different amounts of resources for their differential abilities, but not for their differential efforts, holding ability (the consequence of circumstances) constant.

How can the common view, that equality of opportunity (for educational achievement) requires providing an equal resource bundle to all children, be viewed as a special case of the (as yet imprecise) definition I have offered of equal opportunity? It is the case in which we consider all children to belong to the same type. Then equal opportunity simply consists in providing each child with the same educational resources, and not adjusting for the differential efforts which ensue. By definition, in the world as I have constructed it, any difference in achievement, once types have been defined, is viewed as being the result of differential application of effort or, as I also say, of different autonomous choices that individuals make. Thus I view the different choices that individuals within a type make as relevantly autonomous in the sense of not being determined by circumstances (since circumstances are the same within a type). It is not obviously possible, however, to compare the difference in efforts made by individuals of different types: for those effort differences are in part due to their being different *distributions* of effort across types.

Although I have just explained how the conventional view (that equality of opportunity consists in supplying all children with the same amount of the social resource) can be viewed as a special case of my conception, there are many who would affirm the policy that I just stated parenthetically, yet do not think that all children belong to the same type, have the same set of circumstances. They may believe, instead, that it is inappropriate for the state to counteract biological and social differences by positive discrimination. According to what I have said so far, such people must be viewed as not advocating a level-the-playing-field conception of equal opportunity. They advocate only a partial leveling of the playing field.

I do not have a theory which would enable me to discover exactly what aspects of a person's environment are beyond his control and affect his relevant behavior in a way that relieves him or her of personal accountability for that behavior. In actual practice, the society in question shall decide, through some political process, what it wishes to deem "circumstances." Two kinds of disagreement would surface in the political discussion that would take place to select the appropriate circumstances: first, concerning what aspects of a person's behavior really lie beyond his control, and hence should be attributed to the effect of circumstances, and second, whether to level the playing field partially or fully. I shall return to these important issues in section 3, but here I wish to define the way that opportunities would be equalized, in my proposal, once the set of circumstances, and hence types, has been determined.

Pursuing the education example, one might advocate a set of circumstances comprising IQ, income and education levels of the parents, family type (married and living together, single parent, and so on), and number of siblings. Let us suppose that society chose this set of circumstances, which could be characterized as a vector with, say, five components. In practice, the first component, IQ, would be represented not by a continuous value, but perhaps by five intervals—thus the first component could take on five values. Similarly, each component could take on a (small) finite number of values. This would define a finite number of types; each type, in a nation the size of the United States, would contain a large number of individuals, large enough to be able to speak of continuous distributions of educational achievement within types, as a function of educational resources allocated to those types and of the efforts expended by children.

The process of arriving at the set of circumstances used to characterize type would be a contentious one, as I've said, in which different political, psychological, biological, and social views and theories would be debated. In democratic practice, different political parties would advocate different views, and the set of circumstances comprising type would ultimately be determined by, let us say, the Department of Education, whose chief officers would be appointed by the party in power. The choice of the set of circumstances, however, would be determined not only by different views in the above senses but by the practicalities of gathering information. For instance, many might agree that an important circumstantial variable in the child's ability to process educational resources is the love the parent has for the child, and her treatment of the child. It is, however, neither feasible nor, perhaps, appropriate (because invasive of privacy) to collect such information. Thus the circumstances should be easily observable and nonmanipulable characteristics of individuals.[1] A skeptic might argue against including IQ as a component of type, because a child could, theoretically, manipulate his performance on the IQ test. ("Now Johnny, play dumb on that test the teacher is giving you today.") I shall, however, offer another resolution to the problem of potential manipulability of type in section 5. (Another argument that I've alluded to, against the inclusion of IQ, is that IQ already reflects past effort of the child, and hence is not obviously something for which the child should not be held accountable.)

Clearly, the larger the set of circumstances, and the more finely we measure differences in components of circumstance, the more types there will be. Some compromise must be struck which will keep the number of types down to a manageable level.

---

1. I will relax this requirement later on.

I turn next to another unresolved issue: in what average sense should achievements of the advantage in question be equalized across types? I propose (for the moment) distributing the resource in question across types so that type i receives some amount R_i of the resource per capita, and that the resource be distributed equally among individuals of the type. The problem is to decide upon the values $R_1, R_2, \ldots, R_T$, where there are T types. Let us assume that the society has determined what amount of the resource in question to set aside, so the only issue is how to allocate the resource among the types. There is a set of feasible resource distributions $\{\rho \mid \rho = (R_1, \ldots, R_T)\}$, given the requirement that the total amount of the resource has been preset at some amount, R, per capita.

Corresponding to any distribution ρ of the resource among types, there will be a distribution of effort levels and outcomes or educational achievement levels within each type. I continue to suppose that we can measure educational achievement levels and effort levels. Perhaps achievement would be measured by the score on a test administered when the child leaves school, or perhaps we would adopt, as a measure of the outcome or advantage in question, which is furthered by education, the wage the adult the child becomes eventually earns. Let us suppose that effort is monotonically related to the outcome, within type.

I propose to select the equality-of-opportunity distribution of the resource as follows. For any feasible ρ, there will be a distribution of effort levels in each type: call the distribution of effort levels in type i at distribution ρ, F_ρ^i. (Formally, F_ρ^i is a probability measure on the set of effort levels, which are non-negative real numbers.) Consider persons in different types who have each expended effort levels at the same centile of their type distributions of effort—say, to be concrete, the fiftieth centile. Thus these individuals are each at the median of their type distributions of effort. Since achievement is, by hypothesis, monotonically related to effort within type, and all individuals in the same type receive the same amount of the resource, each of these individuals is also at the median of her type distribution of achievement. I propose that we select a distribution ρ of the resource (across types) so that the achievement levels of these individuals are all equal.

But choosing the fiftieth centile of effort levels was just an example. I propose that a distribution of the resource across types be chosen so that, for *each* centile π, the achievement levels of all those at the πth centile of their respective effort distributions are equal. If such a distribution of the resource exists, I deem it to be the equal-opportunity policy.

Now in actuality, it will usually not be possible to find a single distribution, ρ, of the available resource, which will simultaneously equalize the achievement levels of all those at the same centiles of their type distributions of effort, for *every* centile. In general, for each centile, there will be a distribution of the resource that equalizes achievement levels for the T persons (say) at *that* centile across types. (When I say "equalize," I really mean we seek the distribution that maximizes the minimum achievement level of the individuals, across all types, at the centile in question. Such a distribution always exists. It is the so-called maximin achievement distribution.) Thus we will have one hundred different distributions of the resource, one corresponding to each centile of effort. In section 4, I will propose a compromise solution, which will "average" these one hundred distributions in, I think, a plausible way. For the moment, however, I wish to ignore this problem, and so I suggest that we assume, for now, that these one hundred distributions all turn out to be identical: that is, there is one distribution of the resource, which we'll call ρ^{EOp}, which simultaneously, for every centile π, maximins the achievement levels of all those at the πth centiles of their type distributions of achievement. Since everyone in a given type receives the same amount of the resource, it follows that those at higher effort levels, within each type, end up with greater achievement.

What I must justify is the decision to "level" the achievements of individuals in different types, who are at the same centiles of their type distributions of effort, by an appropriate distribution of the resource. This is the task of the next section. Let me, at this point, simply point out why I do not propose to equalize the achievement levels of all those, across types, who expended the same *amount* of effort, supposing that we have an easy way of measuring that amount (for example, years of school attended might be a rough proxy for effort in the present example). That would be wrong, I contend, because the distribution of effort is a characteristic of the type, and hence is not something the person should be held accountable for. For example, suppose in type 1 the median level of effort is 5, and in type 2 it is 10. The median level of effort, in a type, is a characteristic of the distribution of effort, and since individuals in types should not be held accountable for those distributions, they should not be held accountable for the fact that those medians have different values. But by hypothesis, *where* in her own type distribution a person locates is due to her own autonomous choice—she could have placed herself, with suitable application of effort, at any centile. If persons in different types both fall at the median effort levels of their types, I declare them to have applied effort in equal *degrees*. I thus will distinguish between (absolute) levels and degrees of effort, and declare that leveling the playing field means guaranteeing that those who apply equal degrees of effort end up with equal achievement, regardless of their circumstances. The centile of the effort distribution of one's type provides a meaningful intertype comparison of the degree of effort expended in the sense that the level of effort does not.

§3

Justifying the Proposal

The proposal in section 2 for how to equalize opportunities for achievement implements equal outcomes (there, educational achievements or future earnings) for individuals in different types who expend the same degree of effort, where a person's degree of effort is defined by his centile in the effort distribution of those of his type. (We continue to suppose that we have a direct measure of the level of effort.) I distinguished between degrees and levels of effort: persons exerting the same degree of effort, in different types, will generally not exert the same level of effort. The proposal may seem counterintuitive: should not, perhaps, an equal-opportunity policy seek to equalize outcomes for those who expend equal *levels* of effort, independent of circumstances?

Consider individuals of two types in the education problem, who have been provided with resources in amounts R_1 and R_2. Suppose type 1 consists of black children, living in the inner city, in single-parent homes with many siblings, whose parent did not graduate from high school, and type 2 consists of upper-middle-class suburban children living in two-parent homes, with two or fewer siblings, and whose parents both graduated from college. Suppose the levels of effort exerted by the first type range between 1 and 7, with a median of 2.5, and the efforts for the second range between 3 and 8, with a median of 5. Why are the supports of the effort distributions of the two types different?[2] Children form views about the desirability of exerting effort in school by observing what others are doing and by making inferences about the value of education from observing adults who have and have not achieved education, at various levels, and how their lives have consequently

---

2. The *support* of a distribution is the set of values that are taken on by it: for example, the interval [1, 7] for the first type.

gone. These "views" include their beliefs and their preferences: preferences themselves may be influenced by beliefs, through cognitive dissonance, as in the sour-grapes phenomenon. Influenced by these beliefs and preferences, a child decides what is a reasonable level of effort to exert—some would say an optimal level, but I use "reasonable" as the adjective to suggest that the child's decision process is not necessarily entirely rational or well worked out. When we observe that no child of type 1 exerts an effort level of 8, while some children of type 2 do, I am suggesting that we should conclude that *no* child, were he to have been raised in the circumstances defining type 1, would have chosen an effort level of 8: exerting 8 is just a crazy thing to do, if your beliefs and preferences are those formed by a type 1 set of circumstances. This inference is based, in part, on there being a large number of individuals in type 1.

Thus I take the support of the distribution of effort observed in a type as delimiting the set of efforts one can reasonably expect of a person in those circumstances and provided with those resources. It is not the set of physically possible efforts—it may well have been physically possible for a type 1 child to have exerted effort level 8. Society says that, within a type, those who exert more effort are trying harder, and society attributes that propensity not to circumstances, but to persons' own autonomous choices: for by construction, all those in the same type have identical circumstances. One could, of course, argue that there are other, unobserved circumstances that explain the difference between those who exert effort 1 and effort 7 among type 1 children, but by hypothesis, that objection is, at this point, moot. For the characteristics of type constitute the full set of characteristics that society is willing to deem influence a person's relevant behavior and for which society will not hold him accountable. (There will always be mistakes, of course, consisting in incorrect measurements of circumstances, in the application of any such policy.)

Let us further suppose that Alan, in type 1, has exerted an effort level of 5, which occurs at the ninetieth centile of the effort distribution of type 1 children, and Betsy, a type 2 child, has exerted an effort level of 5 as well, at the median of her type's effort distribution. I think it is plausible to say that Alan has tried harder than Betsy. I take the empirical distributions of effort among type 1 and 2 children to imply the following: that if any large, randomly chosen group of children were to have been raised in type 1 circumstances, then only 10 percent of them would have exerted more effort than Alan did, while if any large, randomly chosen group of children were to have been raised in type 2 circumstances, 50 percent of them would have exerted more effort than Betsy did. In particular, had Betsy been raised in type 1 circumstances,[3] with maximum likelihood she would have exerted 2.5 units of effort, not 5 units. Taking into account their respective circumstances, Alan has tried harder than Betsy.

Finally, I think that under an equal-opportunity policy, individuals who try equally hard should end up with equal outcomes. Since I deem those at identical centiles of their effort distributions to have tried equally hard, my equal-opportunity rule is to distribute resources in that way which equalizes (more precisely, maximins) outcomes for all those at the same centile of their type distributions of effort.

The choice of the degree of effort (as measured by the percentile of effort levels within a type) as the relevant metric for how hard a person tries is justified by a view that, if we could somehow disembody individuals from their circumstances, then the *distribution* of the propensity to exert effort would be the same in every type. Underneath their circumstances, then, persons are not presupposed to be identical—they differ in their propensity to expend effort. What I call the *assumption of charity* says that, within any type, that distribution would be the same, were we able to factor out the (different) circumstances which define different types. The percentile metric is a way of making comparisons, across types, of the propensity to expend effort. José Ortega y Gasset put it well: "Yo soy: yo y mi circunstancia."[4] Underneath his circumstances a person is not simply a lump of homogeneous human clay, but retains some kind of deep individuality.[5]

Thus an equal-opportunity view is, in my interpretation, a desert-based view, in which reward is due to persons according to their propensity to expend effort. I take the assumption of charity to imply that, if two

---

3. This counterfactual might be difficult to imagine if circumstances include characteristics like genes.

4. "I am: I and my circumstance" (Ortega y Gasset 1983, p. 322 [1914]).

5. The assumption of charity concerns a metaphysical hypothesis that many will argue is incoherent: namely, that we can conceive of individuals denuded of their circumstances, and that differences among such denuded persons would still exist. I do not wish vigorously to defend this hypothesis: it is *one way* of justifying the thesis that individuals of different types who expend the same degree of effort have tried equally hard. Another way is simply to assert that the only relevant comparison group for an individual is his type cohort, and hence we must measure the degree of a person's effort by noting where it falls in the effort distribution of his type. This then provides a natural metric for inter-type comparisons of effort.

actual persons with different circumstances exert the same degree of effort, their propensities to expend effort are the same, and they should, therefore, receive equal rewards—equal outcomes, whatever the outcome in question.[6]

J. R. Lucas (1995) makes a useful distinction between merit and desert. One merits something (say, a position on a baseball team) because of attributes one has, but one deserves a reward (say, for rescuing a drowning person) because of what one has done. Of course, one's attributes may be the consequences of both circumstances and effort, and likewise, "what one has done" may be in part a consequence of one's circumstances as well as of effort; so we cannot identify Lucas's "attributes" with my "circumstances" and his "what one has done" with my "effort." But I think Lucas's distinction between merit and desert is useful in our context, nevertheless. In a Lucasian meritocracy, a person would be rewarded according to his attributes, whether they were the consequence of effort or not. Thus a person with a high innate intelligence, who received high grades in secondary school though hardly trying, would gain entry into university. Indeed, all those with high grades in secondary school would gain entry, and only those. Under an equal-opportunity policy, were IQ a component of circumstance, some students who tried hard, but were not of high intelligence and did not receive high grades,[7] would also be admitted. Indeed, were university admissions governed entirely by an equal-opportunity policy, then admissions would be entirely due to degrees of effort, not IQ, insofar as IQ were deemed to be a circumstance. The fact that most of us would not advocate such a policy for university admissions does not mean that my definition of the equal-opportunity policy is awry—it means that we do not think it right that university admissions policy be (entirely) an equal-opportunity policy (or, alternatively, that we would not include IQ in the set of circumstances for the purposes of analyzing the university admissions issue).

I shall next introduce a distinction between responsibility and accountability, one not usually made in ordinary discourse. I am interested in these terms in the sense they bear in expressions such as being "responsible or

---

6. This claim is actually stronger than the assumption of charity, for that assumption only says that the *distribution* of the propensity to expend effort would be the same for all types, were we able to peel away their characterizing circumstances.

7. I here assume that grades reflect achievement, not effort.

accountable for one's behavior." I will view accountability as defining a (partial) ordering on a set of behaviors performed by different persons. Thus one should be able to say, "Jill is to be held more accountable for doing Y than Jack is for doing X," or perhaps more precisely, "Jill is to be held more accountable for the consequences of her doing Y than Jack is for the consequences of his doing X." Perhaps responsibility also defines an order on behaviors, but I am not interested in that.

I will follow Thomas Scanlon (1988) in defining moral responsibility. For Scanlon, a person is morally responsible for a behavior if she decided to do it in a situation where she was of sound mind, so to speak. He elaborates:

> What is required [for moral responsibility] is that what we do be importantly dependent on our process of critical reflection, that that process itself be sensitive to reasons, and that later stages of the process be importantly dependent on conclusions reached at earlier stages. But there is no reason, as far as I can see, to require that this process itself not be a causal product of antecedent events and conditions.   (Scanlon 1988, p. 176)

The last sentence is important for us; translated into our terminology, it implies that a person can be held morally responsible for a behavior even when it is determined by, inter alia, his circumstances (assuming that there will be a substantial overlap between socially defined circumstances and "antecedent events and conditions"). Thus, suppose it were the case that the typical German, under the Nazi regime, did not protest against the treatment of the Jews, even though he knew about it and thought about it. And further suppose that we could determine that his nonprotest was in large part attributable to circumstances (which might include being raised in a culture pervaded by anti-Semitism and obedience to authority). Such Germans would nevertheless be held morally responsible for their nonaction, by Scanlon's definition, supposing that we could credit them with sufficiently critical reflection.

To hold a person *accountable* for an action will mean that he should pay for it—he should, perhaps, compensate others who were harmed by the action, or be penalized by society for it. In other situations, a person who is accountable for a behavior, which has consequences for him, must accept those consequences—society has no moral mandate to adjust those consequences. Now we may, in many though not all cases, think that a person can be held accountable for a behavior only if he is responsible for it. (We do not hold the hypnotized person, who is not responsible, liable for the damage he did to someone while under hypnosis.) But it is the converse that interests me more: holding a person responsible does not always mean we should hold him accountable. Thus, for example, we may decide that an adolescent is responsible for a poor attendance record at school, because she decided to cut classes frequently, but nevertheless not hold her accountable for it, by our taking steps to repair her consequent educational deficit, if her circumstances explained her behavior.

I say that individuals should be held accountable for their degrees of effort but not their levels of effort. The consequence of an action for a person should not depend on his circumstances, but it should depend on how hard he tries. Those who expended the same degree of effort should be held equally accountable for the consequences; since they are equally accountable, their rewards (which is to say, levels of the relevant advantage or welfare) should be equal. We can hold a person accountable for a bad behavior only if it would have been reasonable for one in her circumstances to have behaved better: but the set of reasonable behaviors depends upon one's type, and is, I have argued, justifiably taken to be the set of observed behaviors of the type. Thus, although Alan and Betsy exerted the same 5 units of effort in the educational example described earlier, Betsy is more accountable for her relatively low educational achievement than Alan is for his, because he tried harder. And so under the equal-opportunity policy, Alan ends up with higher achievement than Betsy.

I say it is morally wrong to hold a person accountable for not doing something that it would have been unreasonable for a person in his circumstances to have done. Thus consider type 3, all of whose members exert effort levels between 1 and 2 with a certain resource endowment. It is wrong to say that these individuals deserve educational achievements less than someone in type 2 who exerted "3" in effort, where many individuals of type 2 exerted more than 3. For the assumption of charity says that it would be unreasonable to expect anyone from a large, randomly chosen group of persons to have exerted effort 3, were his circumstances to have been those of type 3, while many of such a group of persons would have exerted 3 or better, had they been more fortunate in circumstances.

The distinction between responsibility and accountability enables us to maintain certain moral standards, with respect to actions, yet not punish the person who performs a bad act if only a superhuman would have avoided the act under those circumstances. Thus suppose the median effort level among type 1 children (always, in the above education problem) involves cutting school one day a week. We can say, "That's a bad thing to do, and we hold you responsible for doing it," yet at the same time we need not hold the child accountable by declining to repair his educational deficit, which would, without further intervention, otherwise follow from the behavior. So an equal-opportunity policy may require providing more educational resources to some children who cut classes than to others who do not, by virtue of their circumstantially determined behavior. (Of course, the distribution of effort—in particular, the frequency of class-cutting behavior—will itself be influenced by the allocation of the educational resource.)

I have said that many would argue that the set of circumstances should coincide with characteristics of the environment (broadly defined) which influence behavior yet are beyond the person's control. But there is a prominent position in egalitarian political philosophy which disagrees. Ronald Dworkin (1981a, b) argues that persons should be held accountable for their choices, even if they follow from preferences which were in part or entirely formed under influences beyond their control, as long as they identify with those preferences. Indeed, the scheme that Dworkin proposes to implement "equality of resources," of hypothetical insurance contracting behind a thin veil of ignorance, is one that is intended to let persons sustain the consequences of their preferences but not of what he calls their resource endowment, which consists of certain aspects of their social and biological endowment beyond their control. (I have argued elsewhere [Roemer 1996, chap. 7] that Dworkin's insurance scheme fails to implement a policy consonant with his philosophical view, but that point is tangential to the present discussion.) The only kinds of choice for which Dworkin does not hold the person accountable are ones devolving from cravings and addictions, preferences the person wished she did not have.

According to Dworkin's view, the type 1 young person who cuts school because she has a distaste for it—a distaste not uncommon among those of her type—would be accountable for that action, as long as she identifies with her preferences, is glad she has them, and sees no reason to change them. (We must also assume that this student has reached an age at which she is deemed capable of autonomous choice.) Dworkin's move, here, is motivated by a fear that not holding a person accountable for the consequences of exercising tastes with which she identifies would risk demeaning the integrity of the person, compromising the respect that society owes her as a person with the capacity to make her own way. But I do not hold a person's identification with her preferences to be quite so sacred—at least, with respect to many kinds of preference. Preferences are often adjusted to what the person falsely deems to be necessity, and society does her no favor by accepting the consequences that follow from exercising them.

There are, however, some preferences that, even though formed under influences beyond the person's control, must be respected, in the sense that society should not try to adjust the consequences a person endures from their exercise. Scanlon (1986) gives the example of a person who takes on a religion which requires of him a penurious style of life, where his adoption of the religion was clearly due to training he received at a very early age. Let us suppose that the penury of his lifestyle reduces his opportunities below the norm, owing to the man's consequent poor health or general functioning. I agree with Scanlon that this situation is not an injustice or a violation of equal opportunity, *if* it is clear that the man's adoption of the religion was not in fact due to circumstances which made penury seem unavoidable, for were that the case, then it would be hard to distinguish the behavior of adopting the religion from the fox's decision to dislike the unreachable grapes.[8] In the example of the class-cutting adolescent, I asserted that her distaste for school could arguably be traced in no small part to her circumstances, which made schooling appear to be a waste of time. If few of her type had school-hating preferences, however, then the consequences of exercising her preferences would appear as low effort, the results of which she would be more accountable for.

Amartya Sen (1985) gives the example of the "tamed housewife" to show the undesirability of taking the welfare of individuals, as they measure it, as the right equalisandum of an egalitarian theory of justice. The tamed house-wife is one who, owing to the apparent impossibility of surviving outside a highly restricting marriage, adopts preferences in which she likes cleaning house, changing diapers, washing dishes, and the like. (Other examples are "the battered slave, the hopeless destitute.") Must an equal-opportunity pol-icy accept the self-limiting views of tamed housewives, because they identify with their preferences, or should it provide resources which might enable them to reconsider their preferences? I think the latter. The question an equal-opportunity view must consider is not simply whether a person identi-fies with his preferences, but whether preferences which attribute low value to certain "lifestyles" were adopted precisely because the person perceived that those lifestyles were unattainable.

---

8. If his adoption of the religion were clearly due to disadvantaged circumstances, then I would take further steps to make resources available to him, although not, of course, forcing the resources upon him, to the detriment of what he believes to be the right way to live.

It must be noted that I am not the first to question Dworkin's partition, which holds individuals accountable for their preferences but not for their "resources." G. A. Cohen (1989) and Richard Arneson (1989) both made the point that Dworkin had misdrawn the line which separates those aspects of a person for which he should be held accountable from those for which he should not, in an egalitarian theory of justice. The present essay, as I've noted, is in large part the result of my reflection on these articles.

I now take up the two problems raised in section 2 that would arise in the discussion to delineate the set of circumstances. First, there is the nontrivial question of deciding when an aspect of the environment should be placed in the set of circumstances, and second, there is the issue of whether to level the playing field partially or fully. Let me elaborate upon the first issue with an example due to Brian Barry.[9] Consider education, and a type of child whom we shall call "Asian." Asian children generally work hard in school (expend high effort) and thereby do well, because their parents press them to do so. They are to be distinguished from children of another type, whom we shall call "academic," who also generally do well in school, although they expend lower levels of effort than do Asian children. Academic children do well because they have absorbed an intellectual culture at home that makes success in school come easy. Let us suppose, in fact, that there is a distribution of the educational resource between the two types that engenders identical distributions of educational achievement (or future earnings, if that is the measure of advantage) for the two types. According to my definition (and assuming there are no other types), this would constitute the equal-opportunity policy.

Now Barry objects that, in point of fact, the Asian students have tried harder than the academic students at this distribution, in a way which calls for more reward than they are receiving. Granted, he says, the Asian students have worked hard because of familial pressure, an aspect of the environment beyond their control, but nevertheless, if reward is due to effort, then they should receive more reward than the academic children, for they really tried harder. The fact that their generally high levels of effort were due to familial pressure does not make their having expended high effort less admirable and less deserving of reward than it would have been absent such pressure.

The issue, then, is whether to include "Asian" as an element of circumstance. If we do not, then the fact that Asian children work harder in school

---

9. In conversation, September 1, 1996.

will be attributed to their autonomous effort rather than to a cultural circumstance, and they will be more rewarded than they would be if we factor out the effect of familial pressure on their behavior, as described in the previous paragraph.

The example is important, for it claims to show that the salient question, in regard to whether effort should be rewarded, is not whether it was induced by a factor beyond the individual's control. There is, it is claimed, something more morally admirable in what Asian children do to succeed in school than in what academic children do. What they do is expend more effort, and Barry says that that's what counts, not that their expending more effort was determined by a factor outside their control.

Although I find Barry's example provocative, it does not convince me that the approach I have advocated—in which "Asian" should be listed as an element of circumstance—is wrong. I think Barry's rock-bottom view is that pain should be rewarded, where pain, in this example, is suffered by Asian children, who put their noses to the grindstone, in contrast to academic children, who sail through. But that is not the rock-bottom view behind equality of opportunity, which is, rather, that autonomously taken effort should be rewarded. If the Asian child does not view himself as having a choice in regard to whether or not to expend effort, because it is simply *expected* by his family that he will, then he is not as morally deserving, under the equal-opportunity view, as someone who expends effort even though he felt no obligation to do so. We decide how much effort the Asian child took on autonomously by comparing his behavior with that of others of his type.

Now to the second problem, which can be illustrated by asking whether we should include IQ as an element of circumstance in the education problem. I suppose, now, that IQ is a measure of pure ability, unpolluted by the previous exercise of effort. Let us assume that a high IQ makes it easier for a person to succeed in school with low effort. The issue is whether we think that those with high IQ should, nevertheless, have greater access to advantage (say, future income) than those with low IQ who applied the same *degree* of effort. I think that many would answer this question affirmatively, in which case they would advocate not including IQ as an element of circumstance. They would advocate only partially leveling the playing field.

There are two reasons (I can think of) for that advocacy. The first is on account of "efficiency": if we allocated educational resources so that low IQ persons ended up with the same future wages as high IQ persons, at the same degrees of effort, then we must have reduced aggregate output below what it would have been had we, say, given the same amounts of resources to high IQers and low IQers.[10] High IQers are more efficient utilizers of educational resources than low IQers in the sense of eventually producing more output valued by society for the same input of educational resources.

I do not maintain that such efficiency issues are unimportant: quite the contrary. But a distinction must be made between what defines the equal-opportunity policy, and whether or not we wish to apply it with full force. (More on this in sections 12 and 13.) I maintain that the equal-opportunity policy requires including IQ as an element of circumstance. Now we may decide to constrain the implementation of the policy, because of the deleterious efficiency consequences it would have in some cases. Not including IQ as an element of circumstance would be one way of doing so.

The second reason for not including IQ as an element of circumstance is that a person might be thought to deserve to benefit by virtue of her high IQ. This is an instance of what Cohen (1995) calls the thesis of self-ownership, that a person has an entitlement to benefits that flow from her personal attributes, in, let us say, a market economy. I claim not that this thesis is indefensible but, rather, that it conflicts with the equal-opportunity view.

There is, finally, a different kind of criticism of my proposal, that says it in fact implements an unattractive kind of outcome equality and thus does not preserve the essential aspect of equality of opportunity, that individuals be held accountable for their actions.

My proposal does not entail that outcomes be equalized for all, but only within particular segments of the population, where such a segment consists of all those with different circumstances who have applied the same degree of effort. I gave, in addition, an argument to justify my way of measuring the degrees of effort expended by those in different circumstances. The criticism I have in mind does not challenge that particular way of calibrating degrees of effort, but rather challenges the claim that opportunities are equalized by distributing resources to equalize outcomes among those who are deemed to have exerted the same degree of effort. I respond that the general view of outcome egalitarianism is only morally objectionable because it fails to hold persons accountable for things they should be held

---

10. I here assume that wages are monotonically related to the amount of output produced by the worker.

accountable for. My proposal endeavors to hold people accountable for just the right things, or just the things that the society in question thinks they should be held accountable for.

Indeed, an opportunity is a vague thing. It is not a school or a plate of nourishing food or a warm abode, but is, rather, a capacity which is brought into being by properly using that school, food, and hearth. It is not immediately obvious how to equalize opportunities, because they are not material things with self-evident sizes. Building identical schools and staffing them with identical teachers in several communities in which children live in very different circumstances therefore will not generally equalize their opportunities for success: the commonly held view to the contrary is based on a fetishist error of identifying an opportunity with a material object that can at best help bring it about. An opportunity, to use Cohen's (1989) phrase, is an access to advantage. What society owes its members, under an equal-opportunity policy, is equal access; but the individual is responsible for turning that access into actual advantage by the application of effort.

A Formal Definition of Equality of Opportunity

In this section I shall propose a precise definition of the equal-opportunity policy in one context. The purpose is twofold: first, I will propose the compromise I referred to at page 11, which is necessary because the equal-opportunity policy, as I have thus far defined it, generally fails to exist (that is, there is no policy that will simultaneously equalize the levels of advantage for all those at each centile of the effort distribution); second, having a precise (mathematical) definition of the equal-opportunity policy will enable us to calculate what that policy is in a number of examples.

The context is that of a "pure allocation" problem. Let the members of the relevant population enjoy a certain kind of success or advantage, which is a function of the amount of a socially provided resource they consume (for example, schools, teacher time) and the amount of effort they expend (for example, how hard they work in school). In turn, both circumstances and autonomous choice determine the amount of effort persons expend. Society has partitioned the population in question into a set of types, $\mathcal{T} = \{1, 2, \ldots, T\}$, where a type consists of all individuals who have the same set of circumstances. (The set of types may be a continuum in some mathematical representations; I treat it here as a finite set.) Suppose the frequency (fraction) of type t in the population is p^t. Society possesses an amount ω (per capita) of the resource to allocate among individuals in the population. Let the achieved level of advantage enjoyed by an individual of type t be denoted $u^t(x, e)$, where x is the amount of the resource she consumes and e is her effort. u^t will typically, but not always, be monotone increasing in its arguments (in particular, in effort). In the example of education, where u^t is the educational achievement of a type t child, it surely is increasing in the arguments x and e. In contrast, the conventional utility function is typically (by economists) thought to be increasing in x and decreasing in e: that is, expending "effort" is done at some personal cost to the individual. This fact, if it is one, is irrelevant for the theory of equal opportunity, which accords desert to the expending of effort, whether or not it is pleasant or painful.

Society must choose a policy for allocating the resource among the population. Let $\varphi = (\varphi^1, \ldots, \varphi^T)$ be a T-tuple of functions mapping the positive real line into itself; $\varphi^t(e)$ will be the amount of resource that an individual of type t receives if she expends effort "e." I will call φ a *policy* and its components *allocation rules*. Thus I assume that every individual in a given type will face the same allocation rule. This is a generalization of what I said earlier, that all those in a given type will receive the same amount of the resource. (That is the special case when each function φ^t is a constant function.) If the individuals in type t face an allocation rule φ^t, there will be a forthcoming distribution of effort responses in the type. We can calculate the effort expended at the πth centile of all efforts expended in type t when facing the rule φ^t. We may hence define the "indirect advantage function" $v^t(\pi; \varphi^t)$ as the level of advantage enjoyed by an individual of type t, who expends the πth degree of effort, while facing the rule φ^t.

Formally, suppose that, facing an allocation rule φ^t, the distribution of effort expended by members of type t is given by a probability measure $F^t_{\varphi^t}$ on the non-negative real numbers. Let $e^t(\pi, \varphi^t)$ be the level of effort expended by the individual at the πth quantile[11] of that effort distribution. $e^t(\pi, \varphi^t)$ is defined by the equation

$$\pi = \int_0^{e^t(\pi, \varphi^t)} dF^t_{\varphi^t}.$$

We then define the indirect utility function as

$$v^t(\pi; \varphi^t) = u^t(\varphi^t(e^t(\pi, \varphi^t)), e^t(\pi, \varphi^t)).$$

As I explained in section 2, the next step is to choose that policy that equalizes advantage across types, for given centiles of effort expended. Let

---

11. The πth quantile of a distribution of X is by definition the value of X such that fraction π of the population achieves value X or less.

us fix a particular centile, π, of effort expended. Suppose we were only concerned with equalizing the advantage of all individuals, across types, who expended the πth degree of effort; we recall that we consider all such individuals to be equally accountable. Suppose the class of admissible policies is denoted Φ—on which more later. Then the problem would be to find that policy φ that maximizes the minimum level of advantage, across all types, of individuals who expend the πth degree of effort for their type. Formally, we write this as

(4.1) $$\max_{\varphi \in \Phi} \min_{t \in T} v^t(\pi; \varphi^t).$$

Call the policy that solves this problem φ_π. I use the subscript π because this policy is the one associated with maximining advantage across types for all those at degree of effort π.

Unfortunately, we wish to equalize advantage across types for every π. If we solve the program (4.1) for each number π in the interval $[0, 1]$, we will generally get a continuum of different policies, $\{\varphi_\pi \mid \pi \in [0, 1]\}$. (If we just let π take on the values of centiles, we will get one hundred policies φ_π.) If, perchance, all these programs yielded the same policy, that would be unambiguously the opportunity-equalizing policy. But this will usually not be the case. I propose to define a compromise solution as follows.

Expression (4.1) is a maximization problem, where the objective function of the maximization is "$\min_t v^t(\pi; \varphi^t)$." This maximization problem is associated with individuals at the πth centile of their effort distributions. These individuals—those at the πth centile—make up exactly one one-hundredth of the population. I propose to give their objective a weight of one one-hundredth in the social objective function—thus, to aggregate the programs (4.1) into one social objective function

$$\frac{1}{100} \sum_{\pi=1}^{100} \min_t v^t(\pi; \varphi^t).$$

The policy that equalizes opportunity for advantage is the solution to maximizing this objective, that is, to the problem

(4.2) $$\max_{\varphi} \frac{1}{100} \sum_{\pi=1}^{100} \min_t v^t(\pi; \varphi^t).$$

If we view π as a continuous variable, taking on quantile values from 0 to 1, then we may replace the summation sign in (4.2) with an integral, yielding

$$(4.2a) \qquad \max_{\varphi} \int_0^1 \min_t v^t(\pi; \varphi^t) \, d\pi.$$

There are, of course, various restrictions one might wish to put on the class of policies Φ. One necessary restriction is that the resource budget balance, that is, that the amount of resource the government is committed to handing out, at the stated allocation rules $(\varphi^1, \ldots, \varphi^T)$ be equal to the total amount of resource available for distribution. But one might wish to place further restrictions on Φ; perhaps one would require the components φ^t to have a simple form, such as being linear functions of effort, or, as I have said earlier, constants.

Furthermore, one might even wish to restrict all the component allocation rules of φ to be the same, or certain pairs or sets of them to be the same. If there were a severe problem of misrepresentation of type, one could solve this by having the component rules φ^t be the same for all those types among which misrepresentation is an issue. Then no individual would have any incentive to misrepresent his type, since doing so would not affect his allocation. Of course, any such restriction would narrow the degree to which opportunity for advantage would be equalized. In a word, considerations of dissimulation (incentive compatibility) may require us to narrow that degree by restricting the size of the class Φ.

Aside from incentive considerations, there are two other reasons one might wish to constrain certain sets of the component functions φ^t to be identical: (1) to reduce the cost of errors in type identification, and (2) to alleviate backlash. Problem (1) refers to the possibility that some individuals may be inadvertently misclassified in the type partition. If the allocation rule φ^t is indeed independent of t, these errors do not matter: in fact, no recipient need ever be asked his type, although sample surveys of the population, where type is identified, will be needed earlier to compute the solution to (4.2). Problem (2) refers to the social acceptability of having different allocation rules for citizens of different types (say, Caucasian and African-American). One must recall that the definition of types is the outcome of a contentious social process. While the politically victorious definition of type, for some kinds of advantage, may count race, for example, as a component of type, there may nevertheless be a backlash if individuals of different types are rewarded the resource according to different *functions* φ^t. (This is not inconsistent with the supposition that the given type partition is the outcome of a parliamentary/democratic process.) So it may be politically advisable to constrain the social choice by requiring component functions be the same for pairs of types which differ only according to the race of their members. More generally, one might decide to allow different component functions only for those types which a large majority of society agrees suffer disadvantage by virtue of circumstances beyond their control (such as the disabled—namely, the differential tax treatment they receive under U.S. tax law).

I must elaborate upon one phrase in the last paragraph. I said that if the same allocation rule is used for all types, then no individual need ever be asked his or her type. To solve the problem (4.2) or (4.2a) for the policy, however, the planner needs to know what the distribution of effort levels will be within each type, as a function of the allocation rule used, because only by knowing such distributions can she calculate (1) what the advantage level at the πth centile of effort is for each type, and (2) what allocation rules satisfy the budget constraint. To discover these distributions, the planning agency will have to conduct experiments on sample populations in which it knows the types of the individuals involved. Once these experiments have been conducted and the distributions of effort in response to the various possible allocation rules are known for each type, then the planner can solve (4.2) for the optimal policy and announce it to the full population. If he constrains the problem by requiring that all types face the same allocation rule, for instance, then no individual need ever be asked his or her type.

To make this point concretely, imagine that we wish to design a tax system which will redistribute income from high-talent to low-talent individuals. If we know the distribution of talent in the population, and the labor-supply response of individuals of various talents to various tax rules, we can find one income tax rule, which all citizens will face, and which will perform that redistribution (relatively) efficiently, without ever asking any citizen whether or not he is talented. Of course, if we could predicate the income tax rule on a person's talent level, we could achieve even more redistribution at less cost, but doing so may be objectionable for reasons of privacy and self-esteem. In like manner, we need not differentiate all the allocation rules φ^t by type, for political, backlash, self-esteem, privacy, or revelation reasons.[12]

This remark is important because, besides showing how the backlash problem can be dealt with, it shows that the planner's informational problem is not an overwhelming one. Granted, it would be a costly task to record accurately the type of every individual in the target population, for complex definitions of type. But if the planner follows the above procedure, that need never be done. The costly part would only involve carrying out experiments on a sample group, in which type is known, to derive the type distributions of effort.

Let us contrast the equal-opportunity (EOp) policy with two other familiar policies, the Rawlsian (R) and the utilitarian (U). The Rawlsian policy is that which maximizes the minimum level of advantage across all individuals, regardless of type; it solves the following maximization problem:

(4.3) $\displaystyle\max_{\varphi \in \Phi} \min_{t, \pi} v^t(\pi; \varphi^t).$

The utilitarian policy maximizes the average level of advantage in the population as a whole. It solves the following maximization problem:

(4.4) $\displaystyle\max_{\varphi \in \Phi} \frac{1}{100} \sum_t p^t \sum_{\pi=1}^{100} v^t(\pi; \varphi^t),$

or, in continuous form:

(4.4a) $\displaystyle\max_{\varphi \in \Phi} \sum_t p^t \int_0^1 v^t(\pi; \varphi^t) \, d\pi.$

Thus I have characterized Rawlsianism as treating all factors as morally arbitrary, that is, as placing no behavior in the jurisdiction of personal responsibility and simply maximining advantage over the whole population. (To make this an accurate representation of Rawls's view, one would have to view $v^t(\pi; \varphi^t)$ as an index of primary goods for the individual at the πth degree of effort in the tth type. Rawls's proposal, that is, is to maximin an index of primary goods, not a level of advantage.) Utilitarianism, in contrast,

---

12. By revelation, I mean that it might not be easy to get honest reporting on some individual characteristics which society has deemed to be circumstances.

maximizes the average advantage over the whole population. (Likewise, to be true to utilitarianism, we have to identify advantage with welfare as the individual conceives of it.)

Let us call the EOp policy (solving (4.2a)), the Rawlsian policy (solving (4.3)), and the utilitarian policy (solving (4.4) or (4.4a)), φ^{EOp}, φ^R, and φ^U, respectively.

Suppose that society decides there is only one type—that is, persons are to be held fully accountable for their levels of effort; then the EOp policy reduces to the utilitarian policy. Thus equality of opportunity is equivalent to utilitarianism, in this formulation, under the most "liberal" construal of accountability, that is, when persons are held fully accountable for their advantage levels.

Moreover, it is intuitively reasonable to believe that as the set of types becomes very large, and each type comes to comprise a very small fraction of the population, the equal-opportunity policy approaches the Rawlsian policy. This fact can, indeed, be demonstrated from the above formulae, although the argument is too elaborate to present here. (Readers may consult, for a proof in a special case, Roemer 1996, chap. 8.)

Thus equality of opportunity has been defined so that the EOp policy lies between the extremes of Rawlsianism and utilitarianism. If we think of different possible specifications of what constitute circumstances, beginning from an extremely "individualist" view in which all behavior is attributed to effort and none to circumstance and moving toward a "structuralist" view in which all behavior is taken to be explained by circumstance and none by autonomous choice, then the EOp policy moves from utilitarianism at the first extreme to Rawlsianism at the other.

In conclusion, I will write, formally, the definition of the EOp policy when there is a problem of potential backlash or misrepresentation of types. Let $\mathcal{T} = T_1 \cup T_2 \cup \ldots \cup T_k$ be a partition of the set of types into k elements, where two types s and t belong to the same element if and only if there is a potential misrepresentation of type t as type s, or a potential backlash if types t and s are treated differently in the social allocation. Then the EOp policy is the solution of

(4.5)
$$\max_{\varphi} \int_0^1 \min_t v^t(\pi; \varphi^t)\, d\pi$$

subject to

$$(\forall j, s, t)(s, t \in T_j \Rightarrow \varphi^s = \varphi^t).$$

This says, precisely, that allocation rules are constrained to be identical for two types whenever there is the possibility of backlash or misrepresentation between them.[13]

We can summarize the problem of associating a particular policy with a given resource allocation problem in the language of social choice theory. Recall that $F_{\varphi^t}^t$ is the probability distribution of effort in type t when facing the allocation rule φ^t. An *environment* is defined as a tuple $\langle \mathcal{T}, p, \omega, \Phi, \{F_{\varphi^t}^t\}\rangle$, where $\mathcal{T}$ is the set of types, $p = (p^1, \ldots, p^T)$ is the frequency distribution of types, ω is the amount of resource, per capita, available for allocation, Φ is the set of feasible policies, and $\{F_{\varphi^t}^t\}$ is the set of effort distributions of the various types in response to all possible allocation rules. A *mechanism*, or a social choice rule, is a mapping $\langle T, p, \omega, \Phi, \{F_{\varphi^t}^t\}\rangle \to \varphi$, defined on a domain of environments, that associates to each environment a policy in Φ. I have defined three mechanisms in this section, which give rise to the EOp, Rawlsian, and utilitarian policies.

---

13. As economists will be quick to observe, the formulation (4.5) is a short-cut around a more precise and general formulation, where, in place of the constraints in (4.5), we write a series of inequalities guaranteeing that no member of any type has an incentive to pretend to be of another type.

Incentive Properties of the EOp Mechanism

Two of the most common objections to the EOp policy, as I have outlined it, are these: first, that it will be too permissive in rewarding low absolute effort levels in disadvantaged types, thus providing poor incentives to members of those types to increase their effort, and second, that it will be socially inefficient in spending too many resources on disadvantaged types who transform them relatively poorly into future productivity (think, for example, of the education example). I will discuss the second criticism in sections 12 and 13; here, I discuss the first.

To be concrete, consider the EOp policy for allocating an educational resource. It will typically be the case that that policy will spend more on children from disadvantaged types than on children from advantaged types. But if the disadvantaged types come to know this, won't they expend even less effort than before the policy was instituted, thus in part (or entirely) neutralizing the effect of the larger resource endowment they receive?

The answer is that they may, indeed, expend less effort than under some other policy, but that does not mean the EOp policy is the incorrect one, or has bad incentive properties. The implied counterproposal of the critic who says the EOp policy has bad incentive properties is that, instead, social policy should aim to maximize the effort expended by the target population. Now this goal can be formulated in a number of ways: say, we formulate it precisely as saying that the desirable policy maximizes the average effort expended by the target population. The desirable policy, under this construal, solves the maximization problem

$$(5.1) \qquad \max_{\varphi \in \Phi} \sum_t p_t \int e^t(\pi, \varphi^t)\, d\pi,$$

subject to the resource and incentive compatibility constraints. Now in general the policy solving (5.1), call it φ^{emax}, will differ from φ^{EOp}, the solution of the program (4.2a). That is, the EOp policy will not, in general, be the policy that maximizes average effort. So what? We are interested in equalizing opportunities for advantage at the highest possible level, not maximizing average effort—the latter view fetishizes effort, making its expenditure a good act in itself (unless it is a confused way of making the social inefficiency criticism, which I shall discuss in section 12).

An alternative way of making this point is to say that whatever virtues the expenditure of effort entails should be reflected in the definition of advantage, u^t. I have taken the view, thus far, that effort is good only because it engenders advantage—thus working hard in school brings about educational achievement and eventual employment at a decent wage or salary. If our critic objects that the EOp policy will discourage effort, he either is fetishizing effort or believes that there are other dimensions of advantage associated with expending effort that have been ignored in the definition of u^t—for instance, that working hard in school builds discipline, which is virtuous for reasons other than for its effect on one's educational achievement. But if this is so, then the achievement of self-discipline should be measured and included, as well, in u^t. The other solution, of advocating a policy that solves (5.1) instead of (4.2a), is wrong.

I have not proposed exactly how the probability distributions of effort in types in response to policies, $F^t_{\varphi^t}$, come about—whether by some optimization process of individuals or otherwise. Indeed, the more generous an allocation rule φ^t is, the lower average effort in the type may be. But our critic might further object that, over time, there will be further "degeneration" in the effort distributions of a type in response to a "generous" allocation rule. To study this claim, one would have to make the planner's optimization problem a dynamic one, where she optimized over several generations, not just one. The principle, however, remains the same as before. The proper approach is to choose that policy which implements equal opportunities over a horizon of generations, taking into account the effect that a policy used in generation r will have on the effort distributions of those in generation $(r + 1)$. It may be difficult to formulate that problem precisely: that is, the intergenerational effort responses to past allocation rules may be hard to know. But there is little reason to assert that, because of these effects, the solution of the single-generation problem, that is, of (4.2a), will necessarily have bad incentive effects. Indeed, it may have just the opposite kind of effect: members of disadvantaged types of generation $(r + 1)$, who see that their predecessors did well (in the job market, say) because of the increased educational resources they received, may be induced to work even harder than their predecessors, under the same allocation rule. Thus the distributions $F_{\varphi^t}^t$, for disadvantaged types, may "improve" over time, as pessimism turns into optimism. The other side of this coin, however, is that the effort distributions of "advantaged" types may deteriorate as they receive fewer resources per capita than before EOp was implemented.

In any case, the correct approach to the incentive issue is to consider a multigenerational equal-opportunity objective, where the effect of an allocation rule used in generation r on the distribution of effort levels at generation $r + 1$ is modeled. It is not to assert, categorically, that more generous allocation rules will necessarily have deleterious effects on future expenditures of effort.

Two more points should be made. First, note that the EOp program, as I have described it in (4.5), is incentive compatible. No individual has an incentive to attempt to misrepresent his type. Furthermore, if the functions φ^t are nondecreasing in effort, then an individual always has a reason to expend larger effort—that will increase his achieved level of advantage. (Of course, he may also derive disutility from effort.)

There is, however, a certain "collective disincentive" associated with the EOp program.[14] If a disadvantaged type is assigned a more generous allocation rule than an advantaged type, that may reduce its *collective* efforts to "pull its members up by their bootstraps" (exhortations by charismatic leaders to work harder, and so on). It must be emphasized that this is not a point about incentive compatibility in the sense in which it is always applied in economics, for the individual incentive to increase effort remains. Balancing this possible diminution in the collective incentive to pull a type up by its bootstraps must be counted the *positive* feedback effects of greater achievement with a more generous allocation rule. If members of a disadvantaged type begin to enjoy greater benefits by virtue of an increased resource allocation, that can alleviate apathy and cause individuals to work harder than before. This, too, is a point not typically contemplated by economists.

---

14. I thank Glenn Loury for this point.

Equality of Opportunity
with Production

In section 4, the amount of the resource to be distributed was taken to be fixed. But in many applications, the resource itself is produced by the population in question, and can vary with the incentives the population faces. A prototype of this problem is as follows. As in section 4, advantage is assumed to be a function $u^t(x, e)$, and the data $\{\mathcal{T}, p, \{F^t_{\varphi^t}\}\}$ are known. We now further add production functions θ^t such that

(6.1) $x = \theta^t(e)$

is the amount of the resource produced by a person of type t who expends effort e. The policy is, as before, a set of functions $\varphi = (\varphi^1, \ldots, \varphi^T)$, where $\varphi^t(e)$ is the amount of the resource allocated to an individual of type t who expends effort e. Facing a policy φ, the distribution of effort in type t is, by hypothesis, given by the probability distribution $F^t_{\varphi^t}$, with density function $f^t_{\varphi^t}$, and so the average amount of resource produced by the type is $\int \theta^t(e) f^t_{\varphi^t}(e) de$; thus the average amount of the resource produced by the population is $\sum_{t=1}^T p^t \int \theta^t(e) f^t_{\varphi^t}(e) de$. On the other hand, the average amount of the resource that is allocated to the population under the policy φ is $\sum p^t \int \varphi^t(e) f^t_{\varphi^t}(e) de$. Therefore the condition that the state's budget balances is:

(6.2) $$\sum p^t \int \varphi^t(e) f^t_{\varphi^t}(e) \, de = \sum_{t=1}^T p^t \int \theta^t(e) f^t_{\varphi^t}(e) de,$$

which simply says that the amount of the resource produced has to equal the amount allocated.

We may define the functions v^t and the three mechanisms characterizing the EOp, Rawlsian, and utilitarian policies just as in section 4.

§7

Equality of Opportunity
for Welfare

In this section I will present an example of the theory. The example itself is somewhat artificial; its value lies in illustrating clearly how the EOp principle recommends a degree of redistribution between what the utilitarian and Rawlsian principles recommend, as I stated in section 4.

Suppose that individuals are endowed with levels of talent, t, that are inborn and beyond their control, but they must choose levels of effort. Let us suppose that individual preferences over bundles of effort and income are determined by a parameter α, where society views "α" as within the jurisdiction of personal responsibility. I suppose that preferences over income (x) and effort (e) may be represented by utility functions of the form

$$(7.1) \qquad z(x, e; \alpha) = x - \frac{\alpha}{2} e^2,$$

where welfare, so measured, is interpersonally level-comparable. The production of income, a function of talent and effort, is given by

$$(7.2) \qquad \theta^t(e) = te.$$

We shall suppose that the distribution of t and α is characterized by a probability measure R on some set $T \times A$ in R_+^2, with density function $r(t, \alpha)$.

Let us suppose that advantage is here taken to be welfare, as measured by $z(\cdot)$. Suppose that the set of feasible policies Φ is taken to consist in the budget-balanced linear tax functions of income, where every type will face the *same* linear tax rule (perhaps for the reasons enumerated in section 4). Denote a linear tax rule, on income, as $\varphi(x) = ax + b$, or (a, b).

38

Facing a tax rule (a, b), an individual with characteristics (t, α) decides how much effort to expend by maximizing $(1 - a)(te) - b - (\alpha/2)e^2$, which yields the effort supply

$$(7.3a) \qquad \hat{e} = \frac{(1 - a)t}{\alpha}$$

and an associated output level of

$$(7.3b) \qquad \hat{x} = \frac{(1 - a)t^2}{\alpha}.$$

Consequently, the balanced-budget condition is

$$(7.4a) \qquad \iint_{T \times A} \frac{a(1 - a)t^2}{\alpha} r(\alpha, t) d\alpha dt + b = 0,$$

which determines b as a function of a:

$$(7.4b) \qquad b = -a(1 - a)Q,$$

where $Q \equiv \iint_{T \times A} \frac{t^2}{\alpha} r(\alpha, t) d\alpha dt$. We will henceforth denote a tax rule simply by its marginal tax rate, a, with b determined by (7.4b).

The next step is to compute the quantiles of effort by type. Let $F_a^t(\cdot)$ denote the distribution function of effort in type t facing the tax rule a, and let R_t denote the distribution function of α among those of talent level t. An effort $\varepsilon < e$, in type t, is expended precisely by those individuals whose α is greater than $((1 - a)t)/e$, from (7.3a). It follows that

$$(7.5) \qquad F_a^t(e) = 1 - R_t \left(\frac{(1 - a)t}{e} \right).$$

Thus the effort level at the πth quantile in type t at tax rule a is $e^t(\pi; a)$, defined by the equation

$$(7.6) \qquad \pi = 1 - R_t \left(\frac{(1 - a)t}{e^t(\pi; a)} \right).$$

Since R_t is an increasing function (it's a distribution function), it has an inverse, which we denote $c_t(\cdot)$. We solve for $e^t(\pi; a)$ using the inverse function, from (6.6):

$$(7.7) \qquad e^t(\pi; a) = \frac{(1-a)t}{c_t(1-\pi)}.$$

We may now compute the indirect advantage (here, utility) function:

$$(7.8) \qquad v^t(\pi; a) = \frac{(1-a)^2 t^2}{2c_t(1-\pi)} + a(1-a)Q.$$

Thus if we apply (4.2a), the equality-of-opportunity tax rule solves the problem

$$(7.9) \qquad \max_a \left\{ \int_1^0 \min_t \frac{(1-a)^2 t^2}{2c_t(1-\pi)} d\pi + a(1-a)Q \right\}.$$

(In this example there is a continuum of types—one for each t—but that causes no problem in applying (4.2a).)

If we define $\tau \equiv \int_0^1 \min_t \frac{t^2}{c_t(1-\pi)} d\pi$, (7.9) can be written as

$$(7.10) \qquad \max_a \left\{ a(1-a)Q + \frac{(1-a)^2}{2} \tau \right\}.$$

The objective function in (7.10) is a quadratic function of a; it is concave when the coefficient of a^2 is negative, which is $-Q + (\tau/2)$. But it is easily seen that $\tau \leq Q$, and so (7.9) is a concave problem, whose solution is therefore given by setting the derivative with respect to α of the objective in (7.10) equal to zero:

$$(7.11) \qquad a^{\text{EOp}} = \frac{1 - \dfrac{\tau}{Q}}{2 - \dfrac{\tau}{Q}}.$$

We can also calculate the utilitarian and Rawlsian tax rules by solving the programs (4.3) and (4.4a). The solutions are:

$$(7.12) \qquad a^{\text{U}} = 0 \quad \text{and} \quad a^{\text{R}} = \frac{1}{2}.$$

Since τ/Q is a fraction between 0 and 1, the EOp rule is more redistributive than utilitarianism, and less redistributive than the Rawlsian rule, as claimed.

Let us further specialize this example by taking a specific probability measure R. Suppose that α ("laziness") is distributed independently of talent: for all levels of talent, it is uniformly distributed on an interval $[\underline{\alpha}, \overline{\alpha}]$. Let the distribution of talent be called G, with density $g(t)$, and support $[\underline{t}, \overline{t}]$. Let $\Delta\alpha \equiv \overline{\alpha} - \underline{\alpha}$. Then we may compute that the inverse distribution function $c_t(X)$, which in this case is independent of t, is given by $c(X) = \Delta\alpha X + \underline{\alpha}$. From the definitions of τ and Q, we may compute

$$\tau = \frac{\underline{t}^2}{\Delta\alpha} \log \frac{\overline{\alpha}}{\underline{\alpha}}, \qquad Q = \frac{1}{\Delta\alpha} \log \frac{\overline{\alpha}}{\underline{\alpha}} \int t^2 g(t) dt,$$

from which we have

(7.13) $\quad \dfrac{\tau}{Q} = \underline{t}^2 \Big/ \displaystyle\int t^2 g(t) dt.$

Thus τ/Q is close to zero when the variance of t is large, and close to one when the variance of t is small, which says that the EOp policy (a^{EOp}) approaches utilitarianism (a^{U}) when the variation in talent is small and approaches Rawlsianism (a^{R}) when the variation in talent is large. This is intuitively correct, for when the variation in t is negligible, then the morally arbitrary element of behavior is negligible and personal responsibility is everything, which should generate utilitarianism, while when the variation in t is large, then the morally arbitrary element becomes important and personal responsibility becomes of vanishing importance, which should generate Rawlsianism.

Finally, let us amend this example to allow the distribution of α to depend on t: specifically, suppose that the distribution of α at talent level t is uniform on the interval $[t\underline{\alpha}, t\overline{\alpha}]$: thus those with greater talent tend to be "lazier." The distribution of talent is given, as above, by the density $g(t)$. We may now compute that $\tau/Q = (\underline{t}/\mu) < 1$, where $\mu \equiv \int tg(t)dt$ is the mean talent level, and hence the EOp rule is given by

(7.14) $\quad a^{\text{EOp}} = \dfrac{1 - \dfrac{\underline{t}}{\mu}}{2 - \dfrac{\underline{t}}{\mu}}.$

Furthermore, it is easy to see that $\frac{t}{\mu} > \underline{t}^2 \big/ \int t^2 g(t) dt$, and so the tax rule of (7.14) redistributes *less* than the tax rule of (7.13). This is as it should be, for in the example of (7.14), part of the excessive "laziness" of the talented is in fact due to circumstance (t): the tax bite on the income of the talented is, in effect, moderated, by comparison to (7.13), because in the second example, the *tendency* of the talented to be lazy is viewed as a handicap for which they are not responsible.

I reiterate that, in this example, the same allocation rule, here a linear income tax, was applied to all types. The virtues of using the same rule for all types are, as I said earlier, the avoidance of backlash and misrepresentation of type. To compute the optimal policy, the planner must know the joint distribution of characteristics, R. I suggested earlier that this distribution could be estimated by sampling. The cost of applying a type-independent policy is that the value of the EOp objective at the solution will be smaller than it would have been, had differential treatment of types been possible.

§8

Equality of Opportunity
for Health

Let us apply the theory to a second example. Consider the problem of financing the treatment of lung cancer acquired as a result of smoking. People in U.S. society have been intensively exposed to warnings about the dangers of smoking, yet many persist, and of those, a proportion develop lung cancer or other serious ailments that require costly medical care. Suppose we hold an equality-of-opportunity-for-health ethic. To what extent should the necessary medical care be financed by society at large, and to what extent should the individual have to pay? If, indeed, we decided that an individual were entirely responsible for his choice to smoke—that society had provided a level playing field by the various restrictions on cigarette advertising it had implemented and by the warnings it had broadcast—then an equality-of-opportunity-for-health view would hold that the individual should pay the costs of medical care sustained because of his smoking, perhaps through insurance whose premiums were an increasing function of the degree to which the insured had smoked.

In this case the relevant effort is the extent to which the person refrains from smoking. The choice with regard to smoking a person makes is in part determined by his circumstances—say, his economic class, his ethnicity, whether his parents smoked, and his level of education—and is in part a matter of autonomous choice. One might question whether "economic class" and "level of education" should properly be "circumstances," since there is an aspect of autonomous choice in determining them. Here is an example, promised earlier, where, even though a characteristic is not beyond a person's control, it might well be included as a component of circumstance. Society might well decide that a person should not be accountable for *not* having considered the effect of his choice of occupation on his smoking behavior. Thus if the list of circumstantial factors for smoking is taken to be

43

(gender, ethnicity, occupation, age), then one type might consist of all sixty-year-old white, female college professors, and another of all sixty-year-old black, male steelworkers.

The social policy in this instance could consist in the health insurance premiums that different persons should pay, where the premium will, in principle, be a function both of one's type and one's "effort"; alternatively, medical services for lung cancer could be financed by taxes on tobacco consumption. These premiums or taxes, of course, are being determined by a government agency whose job is to equalize opportunities for health, not by a profit-maximizing insurance company. We might specify the problem, for purposes of illustration, in the following way. Suppose the fraction of people who contract lung cancer in a given year among those who have smoked for y years is θy, for some constant θ. Let the relevant advantage a person enjoys be given by a function $u(M, y)$, where M is the annual health insurance premium the person pays and y is the number of years smoked. I will specify

(8.1) $\qquad u(M, y) = -M + (1 - \alpha\theta y)\sigma,$

where σ is the "value of life lived for a year" and α is the probability of dying once lung cancer is diagnosed, assuming that it is treated. Thus θy is the probability of contracting the disease during a given year conditional upon having smoked for y years, $\alpha\theta y$ is the probability of dying from lung cancer conditional upon having smoked for y years, and so $(1 - \alpha\theta y)\sigma$ is the expected value of life for a year, conditional upon having smoked for y years. Let us suppose that the Ministry of Health designs an insurance policy under which everyone who contracts the disease will be treated; the question is how to assess insurance premiums on the population in question. Suppose the ministry, for the sake of simplicity, assigns premiums which are linear functions of the number of years persons have smoked.[15] Thus the

---

15. I have chosen to set the problem up as one of determining insurance premiums. The effort variable in this case, years of smoking, is subject to problems of revelation. I shall assume, for the purposes of the example, that the insurance agency can verify years of smoking. Alternatively, had I set the problem up as one of determining taxes on tobacco, then no revelation problem would exist. A person would automatically pay into the medical care fund in proportion to the amount he smoked. This instrument limits the tax mechanism to being one that is proportional to consumption. But see below the discussion of a two-part tariff.

annual premium for an individual of type t who has smoked for y years will be $b^t + a^t y$, where the constants b^t and a^t are to be determined.

Suppose that the "effort" response of individuals to the insurance premium is as follows: persons of type t, who face a premium schedule $b + ay$, will smoke some number of years between y^t and $y^t - \beta a$, where y^t and β are constants, and further suppose that the years smoked, among individuals of type t, are uniformly distributed on that interval. Thus the higher the "marginal premium," a, of smoking for a year, the fewer years people smoke, in general: but the most dedicated smokers of type t always smoke y^t years, independent of the insurance premium. Suppose the cost of treating a case of lung cancer is c, independent of type and years having smoked. Finally, suppose there are T types, where the fraction of individuals of type t is p^t, and let $y^1 > y^2 > \ldots > y^T$. Thus type 1 is the most "disadvantaged" type: its members tend to smoke longer than do those of other types.

We now have all the data needed to compute the EOp, the Rawlsian, and the utilitarian policies. I shall assume, to avoid having to identify a person's type, that the Ministry of Health restricts itself to using the same allocation rule for every type: that is, it chooses one pair of numbers, (b, a), and announces that the insurance premium is $b + ay$ for all individuals. To make the problem more sensible, let us assume that the relevant population consists of individuals who are all sixty years old. (Thus a complete solution to the problem would involve solving the problem for each age cohort.) The data given above are assumed, then, to apply just to the sixty-year-old cohort.

One can, of course, challenge the realism of some of the assumptions I have made in specifying the problem. It is highly unlikely, for instance, that the distribution of years smoked, within a type, would be a uniform distribution on an interval. These assumptions have been made in order to make the following calculations simple. I shall have more to say presently about the specification of the advantage function u.

We first compute the EOp policy, that is, the solution to the maximization problem (4.2a). I first specify the budget constraint. Facing an insurance premium (b, a), the average number of years smoked by individuals of type t will be $y^t - \beta(a/2)$; hence the average premium these persons will pay is $b + a(y^t - \beta(a/2))$; hence the average premium paid by the entire population involved will be

$$(8.2) \quad \sum_{t=1}^{T} p^t \left(b + a \left(y^t - \beta \frac{a}{2} \right) \right).$$

On the other hand, the fraction of persons of type t who will contract lung cancer is $\theta(y^t - \beta\frac{a}{2})$, and so the fraction of the population who will contract lung cancer is

$$(8.3) \qquad \sum_{t=1}^{T} p^t \theta \left(y^t - \beta\frac{a}{2} \right).$$

Hence the cost per capita of treating lung cancer contracted in the population is the expression in (8.3) multiplied by c; so, from (8.2) and (8.3), the premiums collected will just pay for the costs of treating the population if

$$(8.4) \qquad \sum_{1}^{T} p^t \left(b + a \left(y^t - \beta\frac{a}{2} \right) \right) = c \sum_{1}^{T} p^t \theta \left(y^t - \beta\frac{a}{2} \right).$$

This is the planner's budget constraint. We can solve equation (8.4) for the constant b:

$$(8.5) \qquad b(a) = \theta c \left(\overline{y} - \frac{\beta a}{2} \right) + \frac{\beta a^2}{2} - a\overline{y},$$

where $\overline{y} = \sum p^t y^t$ is the average number of years smoked by the most dedicated smokers of the various types. Equation (8.5) tells the planner that the parameter b must be a certain function of the parameter a to satisfy the budget constraint. Hence we may now think of the planner as choosing the single parameter a, where b is determined according to (8.5). Let us say that a must be greater than or equal to zero, and that there is a certain maximum premium, $\overline{M}$, the planner can charge. Thus the largest possible "marginal" premium, $\hat{a}$, the planner can charge is determined by the equation

$$(8.6) \qquad \hat{b} + \hat{a}y^1 = \overline{M},$$

where $\hat{b} = b(\hat{a})$. Equation (8.6) can be solved for $\hat{a}$, once $\overline{M}$ is specified. Thus the planner's set of feasible policies consists of marginal premiums a drawn from the interval $[0, \hat{a}]$.

We must calculate the advantage function $v^t(\pi, a)$, the advantage enjoyed by the individual at the πth quantile of the smoking distribution in type t facing the insurance policy a. π takes on all values between 0 and 1. Since the distribution of years smoked in type t is uniform on the interval $[y^t - \beta a, y^t]$, the individual at the πth quantile of that distribution smokes for $y^t - \beta a \pi$ years. That person also pays an annual premium of $b + a(y^t - \beta a \pi)$. Thus, substituting into (8.1), we derive that person's advantage level:

(8.7) $\qquad v^t(\pi; a) = -b(a) - a(y^t - \beta a \pi) + (1 - \alpha \theta (y^t - \beta a \pi))\sigma.$

We can now substitute the expression in (8.7) into (4.2a): expression (4.2a) says to find the value of a that solves

(8.8) $\qquad \max_a \int_0^1 \min_t (-b(a) - a(y^t - \beta a \pi) + (1 - \alpha \theta (y^t - \beta a \pi))\sigma) d\pi.$

In turn, for every π, the minimum of the argument in (8.8) is achieved at $t = 1$, so (8.8) becomes

$$\max_a \int (-b(a) - a(y^1 - \beta a \pi) + (1 - \alpha \theta (y^1 - \beta a \pi))\sigma) d\pi,$$

which in turn can be rewritten:

$$\max_a \left\{ -b(a) - ay^1 - \alpha \sigma \theta y^1 + (a^2 \beta + \alpha \sigma \theta \beta a) \int_0^1 \pi d\pi \right\}.$$

Integrating, we have

$$\max_a \left\{ -b(a) - ay^1 + \frac{a^2 \beta + \alpha \sigma \theta \beta a}{2} \right\}.$$

Now, substituting from (8.5) for $b(a)$, we have

$$\max_a \left\{ \frac{\theta c \beta a}{2} - \frac{\beta a^2}{2} + a\bar{y} - ay^1 + \frac{a^2 \beta + \alpha \sigma \theta \beta a}{2} \right\}$$

or

(8.9) $\qquad \max_a \left\{ \frac{\theta \beta}{2}(c + \alpha \sigma) + \bar{y} - y^1 \right\} a.$

The solution to (8.9) depends upon whether the term in brackets is positive or negative. If

(8.10a) $\dfrac{\theta\beta}{2}(c + \alpha\sigma) + \bar{y} - y^1 < 0$,

then (8.9) is solved by setting $a = 0$. If

(8.10b) $\dfrac{\theta\beta}{2}(c + \alpha\sigma) + \bar{y} - y^1 > 0$,

then (8.9) is solved by setting a equal to its maximum feasible value, $\hat{a}$. Thus the equal-opportunity marginal premium is given by

(8.11) $a^{\mathrm{EOp}} = \begin{cases} 0 & \text{if } \dfrac{\theta\beta}{2}(c + \alpha\sigma) < y^1 - \bar{y} \\[2ex] \hat{a} & \text{if } \dfrac{\theta\beta}{2}(c + \alpha\sigma) > y^1 - \bar{y}. \end{cases}$

Note that $y^1 - \bar{y}$ is the deviation of y^1 from the average of the $\{y^t\}$. What (8.11) says, qualitatively, is that if this deviation is sufficiently large, then the EOp policy charges everyone the same premium, regardless of the number of years smoked; on the other hand, if $y^1 - \bar{y}$ is sufficiently small, then the insurance policy applies the largest feasible marginal premium per year of smoking.

Let us make a rough calculation of what the EOp policy might be by assigning values to the various constants specifying the problem. Let us measure c and σ in thousands of dollars. Let us say $c = 50$ (in thousands of dollars) and, rather arbitrarily, $\sigma = 50$ (the value the planner puts on an extra year of life is \$50,000). Further, suppose $\theta = 0.02$ and $\alpha = 0.5$ (smoking an extra year increases the probability of contracting lung cancer by 2 percent, and the probability of dying in the year one contracts lung cancer is 50 percent). Then we have

$a^{\mathrm{EOp}} = 0$ if $y^1 - \bar{y} > 0.75\beta$.

Let us suppose that $y^1 - \bar{y} = 10$: that is, the heaviest smokers in the "worst" type smoke ten years more than the average number of years smoked by the heaviest smokers across types. Then we have

$a^{\mathrm{EOp}} = 0$ if $\beta < 13.3$.

Now β is the number of years by which, on average, people reduce their smoking when the marginal premium per year smoked is increased by \$1,000. It seems very likely that $\beta < 13.3$; hence, if these values of the various parameters are reasonably accurate, then the EOp policy would entail charging everyone in the age cohort the same annual premium, regardless of years having smoked. Thus, owing to the constraints we have placed on the planner, of using a linear policy and using the same policy for all types, it turns out that the EOp policy is just the "egalitarian" policy—all individuals pay the same premium.

Suppose, however, that $y^1 - \bar{y} = 1$. Then

$$a^{\text{EOp}} = \hat{a} \quad \text{if} \quad \beta > 1.33.$$

Now it seems quite likely that $\beta > 1.33$, and so in this case, the EOp policy is highly inegalitarian: the premium is very sensitive to the number of years smoked.

We can understand these results in this way. The numbers $y^1, y^2, \ldots, y^T$ are characteristics of the types: thus persons are not to be held accountable for their sizes. If $y^1 - \bar{y}$ is large, that means that a large part of the variation in smoking is due to circumstances, while if $y^1 - \bar{y}$ is small, then a large part of that variation is due to autonomous choice. In the first case, the EOp policy is, correspondingly, egalitarian, while in the second case it forces the individual to be accountable for her smoking behavior. This makes sense.

We next calculate the Rawlsian policy. By substituting into (4.3), we deduce that the Rawlsian policy solves

$$\max_{a} \min_{\pi, t} \left\{ -b(a) - y^t(a + \alpha\sigma\theta) + \pi(\beta a^2 + \alpha\sigma\theta\beta a) \right\}$$

which reduces to

$$\max_{a} \left\{ -b(a) - y^1(a + \alpha\sigma\theta) \right\}$$

and then to

$$(8.12) \quad \max_{a} \left\{ \left(\frac{\theta\beta c}{2} + \bar{y} - y^1 \right) a - \frac{\beta a^2}{2} \right\}.$$

The maximand in (8.12) is a concave function of a; it is maximized by setting its first derivative equal to zero, which yields:

$$(8.13) \quad a^R = \begin{cases} \dfrac{\theta}{2}c + \dfrac{\overline{y} - y^1}{\beta} & \text{if } y^1 - \overline{y} < \dfrac{\beta\theta}{2}c \\[2mm] 0 & \text{if } y^1 - \overline{y} > \dfrac{\beta\theta}{2}c. \end{cases}$$

Thus the Rawlsian policy has the same qualitative characteristic as the EOp policy: if $y^1 - \overline{y}$ is sufficiently large, then $a^R = 0$, and all members of the population are charged a constant premium, whereas if $y^1 - \overline{y}$ is small, then the premium increases with years smoked. Note, however, that the Rawlsian policy is decidedly more egalitarian than the EOp policy, because the cut-off value of $y^1 - \overline{y}$ above which a constant premium is charged is much lower in the Rawlsian policy: indeed the Rawlsian cut-off value is $(\beta\theta/2)c$, while the EOp cut-off value is $(\beta\theta/2)(c + \alpha\theta)$. In particular, if $y^1 - \overline{y} = 1$, and $\theta = 0.02$, the Rawlsian policy would be egalitarian as long as $\beta < 2$, while we calculated, in this case, the EOp policy would be egalitarian only if $\beta < 1.33$. Moreover, even when the marginal premium is positive in the Rawlsian policy, it is generally much smaller than in the EOp policy.

Finally we calculate the utilitarian policy. I shall spare the reader the details: this time, by substituting into (4.4a) and simplifying, it turns out that the utilitarian policy solves

$$(8.14) \quad \max_a (c + \alpha\sigma)a,$$

which is solved by setting a equal to its highest feasible value:

$$(8.15) \quad a^u = \hat{a}.$$

Thus the utilitarian policy is always as inegalitarian as is feasible with respect to premiums charged.

These computations again illustrate that the EOp policy generally takes a middling position vis-à-vis the Rawlsian and utilitarian policies. The utilitarian policy holds people maximally accountable for their behavior, assigning all variations in effort to "autonomous choice," while the Rawlsian policy holds people minimally accountable for their behavior, effectively assigning all variations in smoking to circumstances. The EOp policy implements a position in between these two solutions.

Note that the above computations were all performed under the restriction that the Health Ministry offer the same insurance schedule to all persons in the target population, independent of type. This restriction was imposed to reduce the costs of applying the policy—that is, costs that would otherwise be borne in identifying the types of individuals. As I pointed out in section 4, this restriction also prevents backlash: no person can say that those in another type are receiving preferential treatment. Even with this restriction, we see that the EOp policy holds individuals more accountable than the Rawlsian policy and less accountable than the utilitarian policy. If, however, the ministry felt it were politically and financially feasible to offer different insurance schedules to different types (thus choosing different values (b^t, a^t) for each t), then we could recompute the EOp policy (a more delicate computation, this time), and the resulting policy would be more fine-grained with respect to holding individuals accountable for their smoking behavior. In particular, we would expect that those from more "disadvantaged" types (that is, lower values of t) would pay smaller premiums, holding constant the number of years smoked.

In the problem as specified, the taxing authority is assumed to be able to determine the number of years an individual has smoked. In reality, this is private information, and it would be difficult to base a tax policy upon it. One can nevertheless imagine ways in which an estimate of smoking intensity could be made. At an annual examination, a physician could estimate the number of years the patient had smoked based on a measure of lung capacity; the patient and physician could then agree on a number of years the patient had smoked for purposes of tax policy.

Alternatively, a "two-part tariff" could be levied on the purchase of cigarettes. The first time in a given month an individual purchases a pack of cigarettes, he would pay a fixed tax, receiving a receipt as proof of purchase. In addition, a constant marginal tax per pack would be levied. This two-part tariff would give the Ministry of Health one degree of freedom in its tax policy, just as the tax policy analyzed above has one degree of freedom. The advantage of the two-part tariff is that smoking intensity need never be observed, because the tax levied on each pack of cigarettes automatically taxes people according to their intensity of smoking. The two-part tariff could be calculated to solve the EOp problem.

Finally, the promised comment on the advantage function, $u(M, y)$. As I have specified that function in (8.1), it is not the same as the traditional utility function that an economist would assign to the person, for most economists would say that people smoke because they derive some pleasure from doing so. Thus the utility function should contain a positive term in y, reflecting the positive returns to smoking, and a negative term in y (like the second term in (8.1)), reflecting the risk of death from smoking. One might say that my planner is paternalistic: he is not computing the equality-of-opportunity-for-*welfare* policy, where welfare includes the positive effects people get from smoking, but rather, a policy to equalize opportunities for a certain kind of material advantage, where that advantage is the sum of the expected value of a year of life debited by the health insurance premium paid. Further, the planner uses his own valuation of a year of living (namely, σ), not the individual's valuation, and he does not take account of the fact that individuals have different incomes or wealth. All these assumptions, I think, are justified by a view that the planner in question is concerned only with a slice of the lives of people, namely their relationship to the health-services system. Thus if the planner took account of the fact that the wealth of individuals in some types is greater than that of individuals in other types, and added the person's wealth or income to the advantage function, then these income effects might well swamp the effects of smoking behavior: the EOp policy for that kind of advantage would tend to charge the highest premiums to those with high incomes. Many would consider this to be an unacceptable mixing of different issues: differential income, they would say, should be dealt with by the tax system, where an "equality of opportunity for income" tax policy could be implemented, while equality of opportunity for health should not be concerned to equalize different incomes, but only with the costs and benefits associated with behavior pertaining to health.

I shall, in this essay, continue to propose applications of the equality-of-opportunity idea to slices in the lives of people, for I think that is the way that contemporary democratic societies would apply the policy. A distinction must be made between a general theory of distributive justice, which may entail equality of opportunity in various (but perhaps not all) spheres, and its practical implementation. I believe that progress toward distributive justice will advance at different rates in different spheres—health, employment, education, and income, for instance—and I shall endeavor to discuss equal opportunity as it might be advanced in each sphere.

A response is perhaps appropriate to those who would criticize, from the left, my taking the equal-opportunity approach to health insurance. Many would argue that citizens should be fully indemnified against the costs of illness, with health insurance financed from general revenues. I am, in this section, disagreeing in principle with that stance. I ask these would-be critics: do you not think it appropriate that taxes on tobacco be used to finance the costs of tobacco-related disease? If so, then you, indeed, advocate a policy similar to the one in this section. For such a policy would have smokers contribute more to the health insurance fund than nonsmokers: it would, thereby, hold them in part accountable for their dangerous behavior. The EOp policy is a refinement of that general principle, in which we only tax smokers to the extent that we feel their behavior is not determined by factors beyond their control.

§ 9

Education and Advantage

How should educational resources be allocated among children to equalize opportunity for advantage—say, the advantage associated with income and consumption as an adult? The conventional answer our society gives to this question, as I have said, is that educational resources should be distributed equally across all children, with some exceptions: certain disabled children should receive more resources. There is, however, a minority view that certain kinds of disadvantage should not be compensated for with extra resources, because those resources would have little or no effect on future productivity. In particular, Arthur Jensen (1969) argued that black children have, on average, more limited capacity to transform educational resources into income-producing skills than white children, and Richard Herrnstein and Charles Murray (1994) rejuvenate his argument. According to them, it is wasteful to spend too many resources on black, or more generally, untalented children. (These authors argue that a large proportion of black children are untalented.) If it were true that some children were extremely inefficient at transforming educational resources into future economic productivity, it might be the case that educational resources should not be "wasted" on them, but rather that income should be transferred to them, as adults, from more productive types. (Herrnstein and Murray, however, do not recommend income transfers to less "talented" types; they suggest providing them with meaningful work in the community, presumably at a subsistence level of pay.)

Of course, the viability of this course of action depends upon the political possibility of redistribution of income through taxation. In the extreme case, when no redistribution is possible, then equality of opportunity for advantage, where advantage depends on income, would surely require spending educational resources on all children, and, indeed, spending more resources on children who, by virtue of their circumstances, were less efficient at transforming those resources into future economic productivity. In this section, I will study the following question. Suppose that society has allocated a certain fraction of its national product to educate its children.[16] Children come in different types, with respect to their ability or propensity to transform educational resources into future economic productivity. Within types, children will respond to education by applying different efforts. The advantage in question is the consumption bundle of the adult the child will become. Think of this problem as taking place over two periods: in the present period (date 0), there are children to be educated, and in the next period (date 1), those children will be adults with income-producing skills, determined in part by the educational resource that was invested in them, in part by their type, and in part by the effort they expended in school. Obviously, children who become high-income adults will be able to consume larger bundles and enjoy greater advantage.

I will assume that the planner, in the society at date 0, has two instruments at her disposal for implementing equality of opportunity for advantage of next period's adults: the manner in which she distributes the available educational resource among the present generation of children and the redistributive income tax policy she imposes on adults of the next period, whom today's children become. A policy, in this case, consists of a distribution of the educational resource among today's children and an income tax scheme to be imposed on the next period's adults. The problem is to choose the policy that equalizes opportunity for advantage, defined, as I said, as the consumption of the next period's adults.

I shall model this problem as follows. There are two dates, 0 and 1. At date 0, there are two types of child, 1 and 2. There is available an amount of educational resource, $\bar{R}$ per capita, to be expended on the education of

---

16. What fraction of its income society devotes to the purpose of equalizing opportunities for its children (or for anyone else) is not a question within the scope of this essay, as answering it would require a general theory of distributive justice, from which would follow an intergenerational allocation. The problem I address is how to equalize opportunities, once society has allocated a sum toward that end.

children. The wage a date-1 adult (date 0's child) will earn is a function of the effectiveness of his education, which is in turn a function of the educational resource invested in him and of the effort he applies in school: we write

(9.1) $w_t = \omega_t(R, e)$,

where w_t is the wage at date 1 of a type t child, where R is the resource invested in his education, and e is the effort he applies. Thus ω_t is type t's "wage production function."

We assume that the ω_t are *commonly separable*, that is, that there exist increasing functions h_t and φ such that:

(9.2a) $\forall t \quad \omega_t(R, e) = h_t(R)\varphi(e)$

and $h_2(R) > h_1(R)$ for $R > 0$.

Thus at any resource investment–effort tuple, the earning capacity of the adult a type 1 child will become is no larger than the earning capacity of the adult a type 2 child will become. Finally, we assume that

(9.2b) $h_t(0) = 0$.

An example of such wage production functions is

$$\omega_t(R, e) = \delta w_t^0 R^\gamma e^{1-\gamma},$$

where w_t^0 is the income of the parent at date 0. In this formulation, the effectiveness with which the child turns resources and effort into future earnings is influenced by the socioeconomic status of her family.

Let f_t be the fraction of type t children at date 0. We shall assume that there are only two effort levels possible, $\bar{e}$ (high) and $\underline{e}$ (low). The fraction of type t children who exert high effort is $p_t(R)$, where p_t is an increasing function.

When children become adults, they take on a utility function $u(x, L)$, where x is income and L is labor expended on the job. Thus an adult's labor supply is determined by the usual utility-maximizing calculus.

The equal-opportunity planner wishes to equalize opportunities for welfare, as adults, of today's (date 0) children. She has at her disposal two instruments: the distribution of the educational resource $\overline{R}$ among children, and an income tax applied to date 1 adults. Let us suppose that the income tax has two functions: to redistribute income among date 1 adults, and to raise educational finance, in the amount $\overline{R}$ per capita, say, for children at date 1. Let Z be the family of income tax schedules she may use, and let $\tau \in Z$ be a generic *after-tax* function: thus $\tau(x)$ is the after-tax income of an adult who earns x.

Note that, in the present example, the effort level of children in school is not influenced by the tax regime they will face as adults.

The labor supply of an adult who earns wage w and faces tax rule τ is given by

$$(9.3a) \qquad L(w, \tau) \equiv \arg \max_{L} u(\tau(wL), L);$$

his (adult) indirect utility is then given by

$$(9.3b) \qquad \tilde{u}(w, \tau) \equiv u(\tau(wL(w, \tau)), L(w, \tau)).$$

We will assume that the planner limits herself to incentive-compatible tax rules, so

$$(9.4) \qquad \forall \tau \quad w' \geq w \quad \Rightarrow \quad \tilde{u}(w', \tau) \geq \tilde{u}(w, \tau).$$

We now set up the EOp objective. We have only two levels of effort among children, $\overline{e}$ and $\underline{e}$. It is thus not possible to define centiles of effort. Instead we adopt a more conservative approach, which conceives of the EOp problem as seeking to equalize the adult welfare of all those children expending the same *level* of effort.

Let $\varepsilon_1 \overline{R}$ be the amount of resource expended on each type 1 child; then $\varepsilon_2 \overline{R}$ is the resource expended on each type 2 child, where the vector ε is on the simplex

$$\varepsilon_1 f_1 + \varepsilon_2 f_2 = 1.$$

Thus the fraction of children expending high effort is $g(\varepsilon) = \sum p_t(\varepsilon_t \overline{R}) f_t$, while the fraction $1 - g(\varepsilon)$ expend low effort. Thus we may write the planner's problem as

(9.5)
$$\max_{\varepsilon_1, \varepsilon_2, \tau} \left\{ g(\varepsilon) \min_t \tilde{u}(\omega_t(\varepsilon_t \overline{R}, \overline{e}), \tau) + (1 - g(\varepsilon)) \min_t \tilde{u}(\omega_t(\varepsilon_t \overline{R}, \underline{e}), \tau) \right\}$$
$$\text{s.t. } \sum \varepsilon_t f_t = 1.$$

This is the form program (4.2a) takes in the present environment, where we try to equalize welfare at each effort *level* rather than at each effort *centile*.

The constraint in program (9.5) allows us to eliminate ε_2 from the problem and express all quantities in terms of ε_1. Let τ^* be the tax regime at the solution of (9.5); then (9.5) reduces to a program in one variable, ε_1, where we replace τ with τ^*.

Let us study the function $\psi(\varepsilon_1, \overline{e}) = \min_t \tilde{u}(\omega_t(\varepsilon_t \overline{R}, \overline{e}), \tau^*)$. The function $\psi(\varepsilon_1, \overline{e})$ is graphed in Figure 9.1. ψ is the lower envelope of the two indicated curves in Figure 9.1. Assumption (9.2b) assures us that the curves cross, as indicated. The value ε_1^* is determined by the equation

(9.6) $\tilde{u}(\omega_1(\varepsilon_1^* \overline{R}, \overline{e}), \tau^*) = \tilde{u}(\omega_2(\varepsilon_2^* \overline{R}, \overline{e}), \tau^*).$

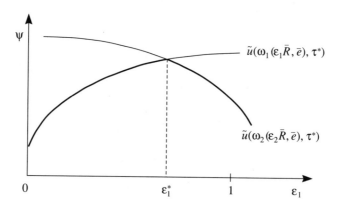

Figure 9.1
The function $\psi(\varepsilon_1, \overline{e})$

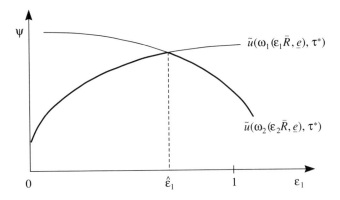

Figure 9.2
The function $\psi(\varepsilon_1, \underline{e})$

Now incentive compatibility ((9.4)) implies that $\omega_1(\varepsilon_1^* \overline{R}, \overline{e}) = \omega_2(\varepsilon_2^* \overline{R}, \overline{e})$, which implies, by (9.2a):

$$(9.7) \qquad h_1(\varepsilon_1^* \overline{R}) = h_2(\varepsilon_2^* \overline{R}).$$

As h_1 increases in ε_1, h_2 decreases, viewed as a function of ε_1, and so $(\varepsilon_1^*, \varepsilon_2^*)$ is uniquely determined.

Next we apply the same analysis to the function $\psi(\varepsilon_1, \underline{e}) = \min_t$ $\tilde{u}(w_t(\varepsilon_t \overline{R}, \underline{e}), \tau^*)$. Again we have the picture of Figure 9.2, where now $\hat{\varepsilon}_1$ is determined by the equation

$$(9.8) \qquad h_1(\hat{\varepsilon}_1 \overline{R}) = h_2(\hat{\varepsilon}_2 \overline{R}).$$

But since ε_1^* was uniquely determined, it follows from (9.7) and (9.8) that $\varepsilon_1^* = \hat{\varepsilon}_1$.

Let us now specialize to the case where the functions p_t are constants. Then $g(\varepsilon) = g = \sum p_t f_t$. The program (9.5) now seeks to maximize the average $g\psi(\varepsilon_1, \overline{e}) + (1 - g)\psi(\varepsilon_1, \underline{e})$. But we have shown that $\psi(\cdot, \overline{e})$ and $\psi(\cdot, \underline{e})$ are *simultaneously* maximized at the value $\varepsilon_1 = \varepsilon_1^*$. Thus the solution to the program is $(\varepsilon_1^*, \varepsilon_2^*, \tau^*)$, which entails:

$$\omega_1(\varepsilon_1^* \overline{R}, \overline{e}) = h_1(\varepsilon_1^* \overline{R})\varphi(\overline{e}) = h_2(\varepsilon_2^* \overline{R})\varphi(\overline{e}) = \omega_2(\varepsilon_2^* \overline{R}, \overline{e})$$

and

$$\omega_1(\varepsilon_1^*\overline{R}, \underline{e}) = h_1(\varepsilon_1^*\overline{R})\varphi(\underline{e}) = h_2(\varepsilon_2^*\overline{R})\varphi(\underline{e}) = \omega_2(\varepsilon_2^*\overline{R}, \underline{e}).$$

That is, *educational resources are invested so that, regardless of type, all children who expend the same effort will have the same adult earning capacity.*

Now we may relax the assumption that $p_t(R)$ are constant functions: the italicized claim will continue to hold, by virtue of the kinks in the graphs of $\psi(\cdot, \overline{e})$ and $\psi(\cdot, \underline{e})$ at ε_1^*, as long as the function $g(\varepsilon)$ changes sufficiently slowly.

The result is rather dramatic, for it can be interpreted as saying that the influence of children's backgrounds on the differential in abilities to combine effort and educational resources into future output should be entirely compensated for in the distribution of educational resources. The reader should appreciate that the key assumptions in the argument are the "common separability" assumption (9.2a) and the restriction to income tax schedules. With regard to the latter assumption, if the planner could tax different types differently, then it might be more efficient to pour vastly more educational resources into the advantaged (type 2) children, and then transfer income to type 1 adults at date 1 by lump-sum taxation. It is interesting that this is never optimal when only income taxes are available.

Although assumption (9.2a) is clearly restrictive, it may be reasonable. It has the testable implication that the ratio of wages of pairs of adults at the same levels of effort (say, years of schooling completed) is not a function of the level of effort.

Finally, let us note that the result generalizes to the case of many effort levels and many types. Adding more effort levels simply adds more terms to the maximandum of (9.5), but the analysis is otherwise unchanged. Now consider adding more types. Examine the function $\psi(\varepsilon, e) = \min_t \tilde{u}(\omega_t(\varepsilon_t\overline{R}, e), \tau^*)$ for e fixed. Observe that at the vector ε^* which maximizes $\psi(\cdot, e)$ it must be the case that

$$\omega_1(\varepsilon_1^*\overline{R}, e) = \omega_2(\varepsilon_2^*\overline{R}, e) = \ldots = \omega_T(\varepsilon_T^*\overline{R}, e).$$

For suppose, contrary to the claim, that the minimum of the values $\{\omega_t(\varepsilon_t^*\overline{R}, e)\}$ is attained for a set of indices $t \in S \neq \{1, \ldots, T\}$. Let $t' \notin S$. Then by reducing $\varepsilon_{t'}^*$ slightly and increasing the values of ε_t^* slightly, for all $t \in S$, the value of $\psi(\cdot, e)$ would be increased, an impossibility. Therefore ε^* is that unique vector on the simplex $f \cdot \varepsilon = 1$, such that

(9.9) $$h_1(\varepsilon_1^*\overline{R}) = h_2(\varepsilon_2^*\overline{R}) = \ldots = h_T(\varepsilon_T^*\overline{R}).$$

But this result is independent of the value e, which is to say that the function $\sum_e g(e)\psi(\varepsilon, e)$ is maximized at ε^*, and the proof is complete. (Here $g(e)$ is the fraction of children exerting effort level e.)

Despite this rather dramatic policy prescription, this section may still understate the necessity of educating disadvantaged children, for until now, education has been assumed to be only instrumental for earning income. In particular, because education is only a path to acquiring income in this model, any individual would prefer receiving an income grant to earning an equivalent income from applying the skills she learned in the process of becoming educated. Clearly, this (conventional) economic assumption is unrealistic: not only do individuals usually prefer to earn income by the application of their skills, so does society believe that it is better for people to earn their income than to receive it as a grant. Doubtless the self-esteem acquired through the profitable exercise of one's skills is a fundamental reason for these individual and social views. Self-esteem, unlike income, is not transferable; moreover, income can substitute for self-esteem, as inputs in a person's production of welfare, to only a limited extent. Moreover, self-esteem is acquired as well in the process of becoming educated. If we take this into account, the argument for expending educational resources on disadvantaged children becomes even stronger. If, that is, we include self-esteem as an argument of the advantage function, and if education is necessary for the acquisition of self-esteem, then the argument for educating disadvantaged children becomes even stronger.

Thus the analysis of this section must be interpreted as showing that, when only income taxation is available, equality of opportunity for advantage may well require expending more—indeed, much more—on the education of less advantaged children, even (and preposterously) assuming that the impact of education on self-esteem is nil.

§10

Equal-Opportunity Unemployment Insurance

Unemployment is a major cause of illfare in modern society, and a person's risk of unemployment is influenced both by factors beyond his control and by his autonomous choices. In this section I study how unemployment insurance should be designed if our goal is to equalize opportunity for that part of welfare associated with employment, unemployment, and their attendant income streams.

Suppose that there are two sectors, the first offering a high wage and a low risk of unemployment (the "primary" sector), and the second offering a low wage and a high risk of unemployment (the "secondary" sector). To be hired in the primary sector, a worker must expend in advance one unit of effort, to be thought of as education or training. The von Neumann–Morgenstern utility function of individuals is of the form $u(x, e; \alpha, t) = x - (\alpha/t)e^2$, where x and e are income and training, respectively, t is talent, and α is a "laziness" parameter. I shall assume that the level of talent is beyond the individual's control, and is treated as the circumstance defining type, but α reflects his autonomous choice. I will suppose that there are two degrees of laziness in the population, α_L and α_H, and two degrees of talent, t_L and t_H, where L(H) stands for Low (High). Thus there are four kinds of individual, characterized by these traits: let's call an individual with traits (α_L, t_H) an LH individual, and so on. The population frequencies of these four kinds are f_{LH}, f_{LL}, f_{HH}, and f_{HL}. (I say "kind" rather than "type" because "type" has a special meaning in this book.)

I postulate that unemployment is random, in the sense of being uncorrelated with individual traits, once sectoral membership is given. The probability of becoming unemployed in sector i is p_i, with $p_1 < p_2$. Workers have no preference for leisure, once employed—effort expended on the job is

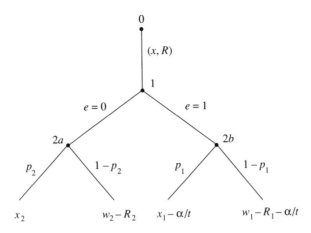

Figure 10.1
The worker's decision tree

not a strategic variable—so there is no shirking issue. The wages in the two sectors are w_1 and w_2, where $w_1 > w_2$.

The problem is to set the unemployment benefits and insurance premiums to equalize opportunity for advantage, when the traits (α, t) are unobservable. A *policy* is a vector $(x, R) = (x_1, x_2, R_1, R_2)$, where R_i is the insurance premium paid by a worker in sector i and x_i is the benefit he receives should he become unemployed. Facing a policy, each worker chooses whether or not to acquire the training necessary to be hired in the primary sector. The "game" is displayed in Figure 10.1. The planner announces the unemployment policy (x, R) at date 0; at date 1, knowing the unemployment benefits and premiums by sector, the worker decides whether or not to acquire the unit of training needed to be hired in the primary sector. He is hired in the primary sector if and only if he receives the training; all workers without training are hired in the secondary sector. At date 2, "nature moves" and unemployment strikes; the unemployed receive the unemployment benefit as their sole income during the period in question. The welfare levels of the worker are displayed at the termini of the tree.

We must, as usual, assume that the utility function measures welfare in a level-comparable manner to calculate the EOp policy. For the sake of simplicity, I assume that the above von Neumann–Morgenstern utility representations are also level-comparable representations of welfare. There are now two fundamentally different approaches we could take: the first approach entails defining advantage as expected welfare; the second entails defining advantage as *ex post* welfare—welfare after unemployment has struck. The first approach is surely more conventional, and I shall study it first. It is, I think, the preferred approach when we believe that the preferences of individuals reflect their interests (but more on this below).

In this approach, the single dimension of type is talent. Facing a policy (x, R), the individual's problem is to decide whether or not to acquire the unit of training. An individual (α, t) acquires that training, which requires expending one unit of effort, facing a policy (x, R), if and only if

$$(1 - p_1)(w_1 - R_1) + p_1 x_1 - \frac{\alpha}{t} \geq (1 - p_2)(w_2 - R_2) + p_2 x_2.$$

Defining $g(x, R) := (1 - p_1)(w_1 - R_1) + p_1 x_1 - ((1 - p_2)(w_2 - R_2) + p_2 x_2)$, we may write the indirect expected utility function for an individual of type (talent) t and laziness α as

$$(10.1) \quad v^t(\alpha, x, R) = \begin{cases} (1 - p_1)(w_1 - R_1) + p_1 x_1 - \dfrac{\alpha}{t} & \text{if } g(x, R) \geq \dfrac{\alpha}{t} \\ (1 - p_2)(w_2 - R_2) + p_2 x_2 & \text{otherwise.} \end{cases}$$

If we recall that α is here the parameter akin to effort, the EOp problem (that is, objective (4.2a)) is

$$(10.2) \quad \max_{x, R} \left\{ (f_{LL} + f_{LH}) \min_t v^t(\alpha_L, x, R) \right.$$
$$\left. + (f_{HL} + f_{HH}) \min_t v^t(\alpha_H, x, R) \right\},$$

subject to a balanced budget constraint, and incentive compatibility constraints, to be specified below.

In the objective of (10.2), there are two alternatives of autonomous choice, α_L and α_H; we weight the two minimization objectives by the population fractions of persons who choose those two degrees of "laziness": the integral in (10.2a) becomes the above discrete sum.[17]

---

17. The same caveat applies here as applied to the model of education in section 9. Because we do not have a continuous effort variable, we cannot measure centiles of effort. Hence, the formulation of the maximization in (10.2) maximins welfare across types at each *level* of effort—or, rather, each level of α. The optimal policy is thus more conservative than the equal-opportunity policy, as I remarked earlier.

I shall now impose more structure on the problem so that we can calculate some solutions to (10.2). I assume that

(10.3) $\qquad \dfrac{\alpha_L}{t_H} < \dfrac{\alpha_L}{t_L} < \dfrac{\alpha_H}{t_H} < \dfrac{\alpha_H}{t_L}.$

Type LH are industrious, talented people, and type HL are lazy, untalented ones. If we take (10.1) into consideration, (10.3) implies that industrious, talented people are the most likely to choose training, and lazy, untalented ones are the least likely to choose training. This is incontentious. I have also set the (α, t) parameters so that under some policies, industrious untalented people (LL) will choose to get training, and lazy, talented people (HH) will not, but the opposite will never be observed. This is a modeling choice.

Solving program (10.2) entails solving five linear programs (LPs), each associated with one of the following cases:

Case 1. Only LH acquires the unit of training;
Case 2. Only LH and LL acquire training;
Case 3. Only LH, LL, and HH acquire training;
Case 4. All acquire training;
Case 5. None acquires training.

Each of these cases can be written as a linear program; the solution to (10.2) is the solution from these five cases with the greatest value. (Some cases may have no feasible policy.) For instance, the optimal solution when case 1 holds is the solution of the following LP:

$$\max_x (1 - p_2)(w_2 - R_2) + p_2 x_2$$

s.t.

(10.4a) $\quad g(x, R) \geq \dfrac{\alpha_L}{t_H}$

(10.4b) $\quad g(x, R) \leq \dfrac{\alpha_L}{t_L}$

(10.4c) $\quad \begin{aligned} p_1 f_{LH} x_1 + p_2(1 - f_{LH}) x_2 &\leq (1 - p_1) f_{LH} R_1 \\ &\quad + (1 - p_2)(1 - f_{LH}) R_2 \end{aligned}$

(10.4d) $\quad x_1 \leq w_1 - R_1$

(10.4e) $\quad x_2 \leq w_2 - R_2$

$\qquad x_1, x_2 \geq 0.$

In case 1, the objective (10.2) collapses to the objective of (10.4); (10.4a, b) together guarantee that LH and only LH individuals acquire training; (10.4c) is the budget constraint, which says that the income from premiums paid by employed workers suffices to pay the benefits of those who become unemployed; and (10.4d, e) are incentive compatibility constraints, which say that the net income of an employed worker should never be less than what she would receive if unemployed.

In like manner, we can write down the linear programs which characterize the other four cases. Given a parameter vector $P = (f_{LL}, f_{HL}, f_{HH}, f_{LH}, p_1, p_2, w_1, w_1, \alpha_L, \alpha_H, t_L, t_H)$, we can solve these five linear programs (on a computer); the EOp policy is then the policy associated with the program, from among these five, that has the highest value (of its objective function).

I shall compare the EOp unemployment policy with the unemployment policy that would emerge if there were a competitive private insurance market for unemployment insurance. I assume, in that competitive industry, that insurance premiums would be linear in the amount of insurance: thus an insurer would announce an insurance policy by announcing two prices $\pi = (\pi_1, \pi_2)$, where a worker in sector i could purchase N dollars worth of insurance for a premium of $\pi_i N$. We must calculate what the equilibrium insurance policy π would be. It is not difficult to see that, because the individuals are risk neutral in income with the given utility functions, the equilibrium prices for insurance will be given by

$$\pi_1 = p_1/(1 - p_1), \qquad \pi_2 = p_2/(1 - p_2).$$

(This is derived by assuming that, in the competitive insurance industry, profits must be zero at the equilibrium.) At these prices, every individual is indifferent between purchasing insurance and not purchasing it. Thus if there were a competitive, private insurance industry, then we might as well say that no worker would purchase unemployment insurance. This is a consequence of workers' being risk neutral in income: it would not be the case were they risk averse.

We can therefore calculate, very simply, the expected welfare of workers if there were a private, competitive insurance market. If an (α, t) worker chooses to acquire the training to enter the primary sector, his expected welfare is $(1 - p_1)w_1 - \alpha/t$, and if not, his expected welfare is $(1 - p_2)w_2$. Thus a worker chooses to acquire training if and only if

$$(1 - p_1)w_1 - \alpha/t \geq (1 - p_2)w_2.$$

I shall now specify various values for the parameter vector P, compute the EOp policies associated with them, and compare the expected welfares of the four kinds of worker under the EOp policy and the competitive private insurance policy. In all four cases, I fix the following parameters as indicated:

$$(f_{LH}, f_{LL}, f_{HH}, f_{HL}) = (.2, .3, .2, .3)$$
$$(w_1, w_2) = (50, 20)$$
$$(\alpha_L, \alpha_H) = (20, 50)$$

I chose the remaining parameters, in the first case, as indicated in Table 10.1. The table also presents the EOp policy for this parameter vector and the expected utilities of the four kinds of worker under the EOp policy and the competitive, private policy. Let us read Table 10.1. Note, first, that there is complete consumption smoothing under the EOp policy in both the primary and the secondary sector: that is, the wage net of the premium in sector 1, $(w_1 - R_1)$, is exactly equal to the unemployment benefit, and the same is true in sector 2. (Recall that there is no disutility from working in this model, so workers whose consumption is smoothed in this way have no reason to quit work and collect the benefit.) Note, as well, that sector 2 workers pay no insurance premium. The entry in the second row, fifth column, of the table is the subsidy per worker employed in the primary sector that is paid to workers in the secondary sector (precisely defined as $R_1 - p_1 x_1$). Obviously there is a positive subsidy in this case, since secondary workers collect benefits and pay zero premiums; the subsidy turns out to be $1,710 per worker in the primary sector (I am here thinking of the monetary unit as

Table 10.1 EOp unemployment insurance for $(p_1, p_2) = (.05, .20)$ and $(t_L, t_H) = (1, 2)$

x_1	R_1	x_2	R_2	Subsidy, primary to secondary
45.8	4.2	20.0	0.0	1.71

	LH	LL	HH	HL
Expected utility, EOp	35.8	25.8	20.8	20.0
Expected utility, Competitive	37.5	27.5	22.5	16.0

one thousand dollars). Although it is not evident from the table, in the case illustrated, it turns out that LH, LL, and HH workers all join the primary sector under the EOp policy, while only HL workers do not acquire training. Indeed, the same worker choices are made, in this case, under competitive insurance.

To continue with the table, note that the distribution of expected welfare has bigger variance under competitive insurance than under the EOp policy. In particular, the three "top" kinds of worker (LL, LH, and HH) receive lower utility under the EOp policy than with the competitive policy, and the bottom kind (HL) receives higher utility under the EOp policy. My interpretation of this fact is that the EOp policy is reducing the "returns to talent" that the competitive policy gives. This interpretation, I think, will be borne out with the next experiment.

In the second experiment, the parameters are the same as in Table 10.1, except that I have lowered t_H to 1.3. Thus there is less of a talent differential in the case of Table 10.2 than in Table 10.1. The differences between the outcomes in Table 10.2 and 10.1 are remarkable. First, note that workers in the primary sector are fully insured against unemployment, although they pay a zero premium. Workers in the secondary sector are also fully insured, but they pay a relatively large premium (over 30 percent of their gross income); the subsidy this time goes from the secondary to the primary sector, and each worker in the primary sector receives a subsidy of $2,500. (In this case, it turns out that only LH and LL workers join the primary sector, under both EOp and competitive insurance.)

In Table 10.2, there is more variance of utility under the EOp policy than under the competitive policy. *Thus it is not generally true that the EOp policy will*

Table 10.2   EOp unemployment insurance for $(p_1, p_2) = (.05, .20)$ and $(t_L, t_H) = (1, 1.3)$

x_1	R_1	x_2	R_2	Subsidy, primary to secondary
50.0	0.0	13.5	6.5	−2.50

	LH	LL	HH	HL
Expected utility, EOp	34.6	30.0	13.5	13.5
Expected utility, Competitive	32.1	27.5	16.0	16.0

be more egalitarian than the competitive market. But the only change between the two tables is that the talent differential is smaller in the second. This forms the basis for my earlier claim that the bigger utility variance in the competitive case in Table 10.1 is due to "returns to talent." In Table 10.2, the interpretation is as follows. There is now very little talent differential, but there is still a large differential in "effort" (namely, the α parameters). EOp believes in rewarding effort differentials but not talent differentials. Because the talent differentials are small in this case, it is fair to say that "most" of the difference in behaviors of workers (that is, in choosing whether or not to get training) is due to effort, and the induced differences in advantage are not to be adjusted for under EOp. Hence it is not surprising that EOp permits large utility differences in this case. I do not have an intuition for why the utility differences are greater than in the competitive case—this is a bit of a surprise. Note that the subsidy goes from secondary to primary workers now: recalling that primary workers are, essentially, those who exerted more effort (since talent differences are small), this is the way that EOp rewards high-effort individuals.

In the third example, reported in Table 10.3, all parameters are as in Table 10.2 except the probability of becoming unemployed in the primary sector has doubled to .10. The change from the case of Table 10.2 to 10.3 is bad luck for workers in the primary sector—an increase in their unemployment rate. But none of the personal characteristics of the workers has changed. The EOp policy responds to this change by increasing the per capita subsidy that primary workers receive from secondary workers, to \$4,730. It turns out that the distribution of worker-types is the same here as in Table 10.2: that is, only LH and LL workers acquire training.

Table 10.3 EOp unemployment insurance for $(p_1, p_2) = (.10, .20)$ and $(t_L, t_H) = (1, 1.3)$

x_1	R_1	x_2	R_2	Subsidy, primary to secondary
49.7	0.3	11.3	8.7	−4.73

	LH	LL	HH	HL
Expected utility, EOp	34.3	29.7	11.3	11.3
Expected utility, Competitive	29.6	25.0	16.0	16.0

Table 10.4   EOp unemployment insurance for $(p_1, p_2) = (.05, .20)$ and $(t_L, t_H) = (1, 2.4)$

x_1	R_1	x_2	R_2	Subsidy, primary to secondary
45.8	4.2	20.0	0.0	1.71

	LH	LL	HH	HL
Expected utility, EOp	37.4	25.8	25.0	20.0
Expected utility, Competitive	39.2	27.5	26.7	16.0

In the final experiment the parameters are as in Table 10.2, except that now the talent differential is much greater than before: $t_H = 2.4$. In this case, the EOp policy views the differences in sectoral choice of workers as largely due to their talent differentials, and this should be compensated for. Hence as Table 10.4 shows, the secondary sector workers receive full insurance and pay no premium. It turns out that here only the HL workers join the secondary sector, under both the EOp and the competitive regime. There is a subsidy of $1,710 per primary sector worker to the secondary sector, which works out to a subsidy of $3,990 per secondary sector worker. Now, as in the case of Table 10.1, the welfare variance is larger under the competitive regime than under the EOp regime.

In summarizing, one should note that the EOp policy can only imperfectly implement the equality-of-opportunity goal of leveling differences that are due to talent but not due to effort, because neither talent nor effort can be explicitly recognized by the policy: the only action upon which the insurance policy can depend is the sectoral choice of the worker. It is worth noting, finally, that in all four cases I have examined here, the sectoral distribution of workers is the same under the EOp and the competitive insurance markets. Consequently, *GNP will be the same under the two regimes*. Thus, in these cases at least, implementing an EOp policy is done with no sacrifice of output. This will not generally be the case when implementing EOp policies, but these examples show that it will sometimes be the case.

At the beginning of this section I referred to a second possible approach, in which the planner defines advantage not as expected utility, but as ex post utility—utility, that is, after unemployment has struck. Why might this be an attractive approach? Because, one might say, whether or not one becomes unemployed, once having made the decision to enter a sector, is entirely a matter of circumstance beyond one's control. In the second approach, the planner would employ an advantage function $\bar{v}^t(\alpha, x, R, E)$, where (x, R) is the policy and E equals one or zero depending upon whether the worker is employed or unemployed, respectively; $\bar{v}^t(\alpha, x, R, E)$ is the ex post welfare of a worker with characteristics (α, t) who optimizes when facing a given policy (x, R) and ultimately enjoys employment status E. (For example, for a primary sector worker who becomes unemployed, $\bar{v} = -(\alpha/t) + x_1$; for an employed primary sector worker, $\bar{v} = w_1 - R_1 - (\alpha/t)$; for an unemployed secondary sector worker, $\bar{v} = x_2$.) Facing a benefits policy (x, R), each worker makes her training choice by evaluating expected utility, just as before, but society no longer takes expected utility to be the relevant advantage.

The EOp objective function now becomes

$$
(10.5) \quad \max_{x, R} \left\{ (f_{LL} + f_{LH}) \min_{t, E} \bar{v}^t(\alpha_L, x, R, E) \right.
$$
$$
\left. + (f_{HL} + f_{HH}) \min_{t, E} \bar{v}^t(\alpha_H, x, R, E) \right\}.
$$

Note that "type"—that is, the vector of characteristics which comprises circumstances—is now two dimensional, consisting of talent (t) and employment status (E). As before, the single volitional variable is α. Thus each minimization operator in (10.5) has four arguments.

We could solve for the EOp policy, under this construal of advantage, as before: the solution would entail solving a set of linear programs, and taking the one yielding the greatest value. But I shall not do so here. Indeed, I would not generally defend taking ex post utility as the proper construal of advantage, if we believe that the individuals in question are maximizing expected utility in their decision making. For when maximizing expected utility, workers would be taking into account the dangers of unemployment, and if we wish to respect their attitudes toward risk, then the planner should not act as if their advantage were properly measured by ex post utility. I might put the point this way: if we take the view that a person's attitude toward risk is an aspect of her autonomous volition, rather than her circumstances, then we should let individuals bear the cost of those attitudes, and consequently construe advantage as expected utility. If, on the contrary, we thought that risk attitudes were an element of circumstance, then we should define type to have "risk propensity" as one of its components. But in either case, advantage should be construed as ex ante utility.

In the example I have studied in this section, the issue does not pose itself in a sharp way, because all individuals are presumed to have the same propensity to take risks in money income—they are all risk neutral. Were individuals to have different risk-aversion characteristics, the question would then arise whether we wanted to view those propensities as a dimension of type (and therefore adjust outcomes to the extent that they were due to different risk propensities) or of autonomous volition. But even in cases in which we viewed risk propensity as an element of circumstance, I do not think it would be correct to construe advantage as ex post utility, for were the planner to do so, she would be effectively ignoring the individuals' conceptions of welfare. One consequence of doing so would be that the planner could propose a policy workers would unanimously find to be inferior to another feasible policy.

Despite these considerations, it is interesting to note that, even though individuals are risk neutral in money income, the EOp policy, in the four cases examined in this section, delivers complete income smoothing over the two possible states of employment and unemployment. So society need not be concerned, if it adopts the expected-utility construal of advantage, that some unemployed workers would starve. Of course, were starvation a consequence of not receiving income in the unemployed state, then we can suppose workers would be sufficiently risk averse to protect themselves in the unemployed state. Postulating, as I have in this section, that workers are risk neutral in income is also effectively postulating that workers have alternative income sources, if unemployed, that are here taken as given, for otherwise we may assume that the utility function would display very high marginal utility of income for low amounts of income.

Even if the present case of unemployment insurance is not one where I would recommend differentiating between the individual's welfare and advantage, there are clearly kinds of social policy in which a paternalistic approach would be called for, such as when individuals have preferences they wish they did not have—addictions are a case in point. If we were considering the problem of equalizing opportunity for rehabilitation from drug addiction, where that addiction is a consequence of social factors beyond one's control, a physical propensity to addiction beyond one's control, and will power within one's control, it would probably be appropriate for the benefit agency to choose advantage as ex post welfare, while the individual in question uses other preferences in deciding whether or not to take drugs.[18]

---

18. This example was suggested to me by Carmen Beviá.

I have, in this essay, taken the position that society will generally choose advantage to be different from the welfare that the individuals in the target population are maximizing. I have not studied when this is appropriate and when it is not. For instance, in the case of lung cancer insurance studied in section 8, society's construal of advantage and the welfare individuals maximize are different (because smoking enters only negatively into advantage, as there defined, but it enters both positively and negatively into welfare, or else no one would smoke).

§11

The EOp Distribution
of Educational Finance in the
United States

In sections 7, 8, 9, and 10, I have analyzed various prototype problems in order to develop the reader's feeling for how the EOp mechanism works. In this section I shall provide a general solution for a canonical EOp problem and then apply it to calculate empirically the distribution of educational resources that would equalize opportunity for future earning capacity between black and white men in the United States.

The canonical EOp problem is to distribute a fixed amount of a resource among individuals belonging to T types, distributed in the population according to frequencies $\{p^t\}$. We may formulate this as follows:

$$
(11.1) \quad \max_{(x^1, \dots, x^T)} \int_0^1 \min_t v^t(\pi, x^t) d\pi
$$

$$
\text{s.t.} \ \sum p^t x^t = R.
$$

Here R is the per capita social endowment of the resource devoted to the acquisition of the advantage in question. In terms of (4.2a), the allocation rules $\varphi^t(e)$ are the constant functions x^t. Thus every person in a given type shall receive the same amount of the resource.

In this section, I show how to solve (11.1) for the special case when the functions v^t are linear in π and concave in x^t. Let us assume that the $\{v^t\}$ have these properties from now on.

The function $V(\pi; x) := \min_t v^t(\pi, x^t)$ is a lower envelope of the functions $v^t(\pi, x^t)$. If the solution of (11.1) entails $x^t > 0$ for all t, then every function v^t intersects $V(\cdot)$ in an interval—for if, for some t, $v^t(\pi, x^t) > V(\pi)$ for all π, then we could further transfer resources from type t to the other types, thus raising the value of the objective in (10.1). (I am assuming that the v^t are continuous functions, and monotone increasing in x^t.) Let us, to simplify

74

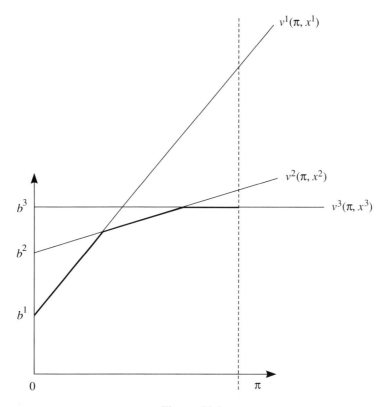

Figure 11.1
The objective function of the EOp program for $T = 3$

matters, restrict ourselves to problems that admit an interior solution ($x^t > 0$ for all t). Figure 11.1 illustrates the situation with three types, when the functions v^t are linear in π.

The bold line in the figure is the graph of $V(\pi; x)$, at a fixed vector x. Because the functions v^t are linear in π, each will intersect the lower envelope in exactly one interval at the optimum x, as illustrated. At the optimum, there are numbers $\pi_1, \pi_2, \ldots, \pi_{T-1}$ in $[0, 1)$ such that, under a suitable re-indexing:

$$v^1(\pi, x^1) = V(\pi; x) \quad \text{for } \pi \in [0, \pi_1]$$
$$v^2(\pi, x^2) = V(\pi; x) \quad \text{for } \pi \in [\pi_1, \pi_2]$$
$$\vdots$$
$$v^T(\pi, x^T) = V(\pi; x) \quad \text{for } \pi \in [\pi_{T-1}, 1].$$

In particular, we have the equations:

$$v^1(\pi_1, x^1) = v^2(\pi_1, x^2)$$
$$v^2(\pi_2, x^2) = v^3(\pi_2, x^3)$$

(11.2)

$$\vdots$$

$$v^{T-1}(\pi_{T-1}, x^{T-1}) = v^T(\pi_{T-1}, x^T)$$

The value of (11.1) at the solution $(x^1, \ldots, x^T)$ is

$$\int_0^{\pi_1} v^1(\pi, x^1)d\pi + \int_{\pi_1}^{\pi_2} v^2(\pi, x^2)d\pi + \cdots + \int_{\pi_{T-1}}^1 v^T(\pi, x^T)d\pi.$$

Now consider a small perturbation which increases x^1 to $x^1 + \delta$ and reduces x^2, accordingly, to $x^2 - (p^1\delta/p^2)$. Such a perturbation is feasible (satisfies the budget constraint). Define the function

$$\Theta_1(\delta) = \int_{\pi_0}^{\pi_1(\delta)} v^1(\pi, x^1 + \delta)d\pi + \int_{\pi_1(\delta)}^{\pi_2(\delta)} v^2\left(\pi, x^2 - \frac{p^1\delta}{p^2}\right)d\pi$$

(11.3)

$$+ \int_{\pi_2(\delta)}^{\pi_3} v^3(\pi, x^3)d\pi + \cdots + \int_{\pi_{T-1}}^1 v^T(\pi, x^T)d\pi,$$

where $\pi_1(\delta)$ and $\pi_2(\delta)$ are the new points of intersection of $v^1(\cdot, x^1 + \delta)$ with $v^2(\cdot, x^2 - (p^1\delta/p^2))$ and $v^2(\cdot, x^2 - (p^1\delta/p^2))$ with $v^3(\cdot, x^3)$. Since $\Theta_1(0)$ is the value of program (11.1), zero must be maximum of $\Theta_1(\delta)$: hence $\Theta_1'(0) = 0$. Differentiating $\Theta_1(\delta)$ with respect to δ and setting the derivative equal to zero yields, after manipulation:

(11.4)

$$\frac{\int_0^{\pi_1} \dfrac{\partial v^1}{\partial x}(\pi, x^1)d\pi}{\int_{\pi_1}^{\pi_2} \dfrac{\partial v^2}{\partial x}(\pi, x^2)d\pi} = \frac{p^1}{p^2}.$$

Similarly, we may define

$$\Theta_2(\delta) = \int_0^{\pi_1(\delta)} v^1(\pi, x^1 + \delta) d\pi + \int_{\pi_1(\delta)}^{\pi_2(\delta)} v^2(\pi, x^2) d\pi$$

$$+ \int_{\pi_2(\delta)}^{\pi_3(\delta)} v^3 \left(\pi, x^3 - \frac{p^1 \delta}{p^3} \right) d\pi + \int_{\pi_3(\delta)}^{\pi_4} v^4(\pi, x^4) d\pi$$

$$+ \cdots + \int_{\pi_{T-1}}^1 v^T(\pi, x^T) d\pi,$$

a variation that corresponds to perturbing the first and third segments of the lower envelope. Again, we must have $\Theta_2'(0) = 0$, which implies

(11.5)
$$\frac{\displaystyle\int_0^{\pi_1} \frac{\partial v^1}{\partial x}(\pi, x^1) d\pi}{\displaystyle\int_{\pi_2}^{\pi_3} \frac{\partial v^3}{\partial x}(\pi, x^3) d\pi} = \frac{p^1}{p^3}.$$

In like manner, we can deduce the following $T - 1$ first-order conditions:

$$\frac{\displaystyle\int_0^{\pi_1} \frac{\partial v^1}{\partial x}(\pi, x^1) d\pi}{\displaystyle\int_{\pi_t}^{\pi_{t+1}} \frac{\partial v^{t+1}}{\partial x}(\pi, x^{t+1}) d\pi} = \frac{p^1}{p^{t+1}}, \qquad t = 1, \ldots, T - 1,$$

where $\pi_T \equiv 1$. These $T - 1$ equations, plus the $T - 1$ equations displayed in (11.2), plus the budget constraint, comprise $2T - 1$ equations in the $2T - 1$ unknowns $x^1, \ldots, x^T, \pi_1, \ldots, \pi_{T-1}$. These $2T - 1$ equations must hold at a (nonsingular) interior solution[19] of (11.1).

Finally, note that the objective of (11.1) is a concave function of the vector x if the functions v^t are concave in x. (This follows because the min operator preserves concavity in x, and the integral is a linear operator.) Therefore, if we find a point $(x^1, \ldots, x^T, \pi_1, \ldots, \pi_{T-1})$ for which the first-order conditions that I have derived are satisfied, then we have found the global maximum of the program (11.1).

---

19. A singular solution is one in which some function v^t is tangent to the lower envelope in just one point. We may safely ignore this possibility.

To fully characterize the solution, it is left only to determine the order in which the $\{v^t\}$ intersect the lower envelope. There is an algorithm for determining this, which, in the interest of simplicity, I will not describe here.[20]

Julian Betts and I are undertaking an empirical project to calculate what the distribution of educational resources among types of children should be in order to equalize opportunities for future earning power. I now describe a preliminary result of this work. We used the second wave of the National Longitudinal Study of Youth (NLSY) data set, and looked at young men. We divided young men into just two types, black and white ($T = 2$). We took $v^t(\pi, x)$ to be the natural logarithm of weekly earnings of men (aged 30) at the πth quantile of "effort" of type t who attended school districts in which per capita student expenditure was x dollars per annum.[21] We measured effort by the years of school completed. (Thus an individual will not be held responsible for the *distribution* of years of education completed in his type, but will be held responsible for where on that distribution he "chooses" to be.) We took $p^W = .85$ and $p^B = .15$.

The first step is to estimate econometrically the functions v^t. We assumed that these functions take the form:

$$(11.6) \qquad v^t(\pi, x) = (a_{1t}x + a_{2t})\pi + b_{1t}x + b_{2t}.$$

Note that v^t is linear in π and linear in x, so the first-order conditions that I have calculated above are necessary and sufficient for an interior solution.

In order to assign each individual a π value, we divided the interval of observed expenditures x, for a given type, into small subintervals, and within each subinterval, assigned individuals π values based on the number of years of education they completed when compared with others in their

---

20. The key is to note that the order of the segments on the lower envelope is the same as the order of the intersection of the functions v^t with the ordinal axis (see Figure 11.1), for v^t linear in π. (For example, the first segment on the lower envelope belongs to the function that intersects the ordinal axis at the lowest such intersection.) The aforementioned algorithm exploits this fact.

21. We took the logarithm of earnings as the construal of advantage in an attempt to capture the welfare value of earnings; we looked at weekly earnings, rather than annual earnings, to capture a measure of earning capacity not polluted by the labor-leisure choice.

Table 11.1 Regression coefficients for Equation (10.6), with standard errors

	a_1	a_2	b_1	b_2
Black	0.0	.331108	.000130	9.993
		(.028)	(.00005)	(.032)
White	−.000317	.443926	.000326	10.213
	(.000007)	(.043)	(.00004)	(.025)

Table 11.2 EOp educational expenditures, black and white males

R	x^W	x^B	π_1
$600	$254.54	$2,557.58	.785
800	467.55	2,683.90	.785
1,000	680.55	2,810.23	.785
1,200	893.55	2,936.55	.785

subinterval. Thus every individual i in the sample was represented by a 4-tuple (type$_i$, wage$_i$, x_i, π_i). We calculated the coefficients a_{1t}, a_{2t}, b_{1t}, and b_{2t}, for $t = $ B, W, by least-squares regression. The results are presented in Table 11.1.

We assigned a value of zero to the coefficient a_{1B}, as its value was not significantly different from zero in the initial regression. Note that the elasticity of earnings with respect to years of education is large (reflected in the large values of a_{2t}), but the effect of increasing per capita annual expenditures is small (the value of b_{1t}). It is a well-known fact that statistical analysis does not exhibit a large positive elasticity of earnings with respect to educational expenditures in the United States. (For a review and analysis of this literature, see Betts 1996.)

According to the optimization analysis earlier in this section, we solved the three (that is, $2T - 1$) relevant equations in the three unknowns x^W, x^B, and π_1, where x^W (x^B) is the optimal per capita expenditure on white (black) students by the EOp policy. Table 11.2 reports the solution for various values of R.

In the mid-1960s, when the young men in the NLSY sample attended secondary school, per capita expenditures nationally in the United States were approximately $600. To have achieved equality of opportunity for future earning capacity (as measured by the logarithm of earnings at age 30), approximately ten times as much should have been invested in the education of blacks as of whites, according to Table 11.2. Today, real per capita public school expenditures have perhaps doubled; thus, assuming the coefficients of the model are unchanged, at an annual per capita student expenditure of $1,200, approximately $900 should be spent on educating each white and $2,900 on educating each black student.

In Figure 11.2, I graph the functions $v^B(\pi, x^B)$ and $v^W(\pi, x^W)$ at the optimal values x^W and x^B for $R = 600$. From Figure 11.2, the reader may see that, at the optimum, the black and white earnings schedules are, in fact, quite close for all π. The white curve lies on the lower envelope ($V(\pi; x)$) for $\pi < .785$; the black curve lies on the lower envelope for $\pi > .785$.

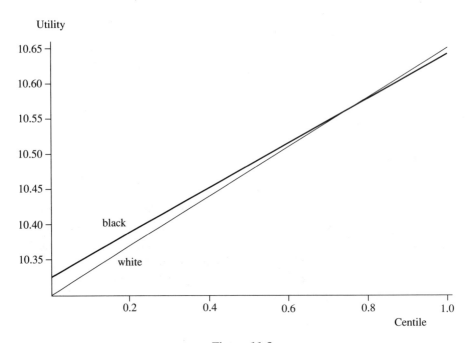

Figure 11.2
Natural logarithm of weekly earnings in cents, black and white males,
under the EOp policy

The numbers in Table 11.2 are dramatic, to say the least. They must be taken with a grain of salt, because the per capita investments recommended are often outside the range of the observed investments, so the linear regressions are not necessarily robust at those levels. A safe statement is that, in order to have equalized opportunities for future earning capacity in the mid-1960s, a great deal more should have been spent for each black student than for each white student.

The large differences in x^W and x^B in the table are due to the concurrence of two statistical facts: first, the large discrepancies between black and white earnings at each given level of per capita educational expenditures and, second, the small elasticity of earnings with respect to educational expenditures, a fact noted above. Yet, despite the caveat in the second sentence of the previous paragraph, it is noteworthy that the theory of equal opportunity here presented requires a great deal of compensatory expenditures, even when we partition society into just two types. Individuals are, in the black-white type partition, implicitly held responsible for the effect of their family backgrounds, their IQs, and so on, on future earnings, except to the extent that these characteristics are captured in being "black" or "white." (For example, if high IQ students attend school for more years than low IQ students, this will show up as a greater degree of effort expended by the former, which will be rewarded by the EOp policy.) In future work, Betts and I plan to disaggregate the sample into more types, to use different measures of effort than years of school attended, and to use different measures of the educational resource than educational finance (for example, class size).

I note that, as well as estimating equation (11.6), we estimated a specification of v^t which had, in addition to the terms in (11.6), a π^2 term. The v^t functions were then, of course, quadratic in π, and so the simple analysis of the solution of (11.1) no longer holds—it is not necessarily the case that each v^t function will intersect the lower envelope exactly once. But analysis is still possible, because the first-order conditions derived above are general (that is, they do not depend on the linearity of v^t in π); it turns out that v^W intersects v^B twice at the optimum in the quadratic formulation! At the optimum for $R = \$600$, the values of x^W and x^B differed from those in Table 11.2 by less than \$1. We therefore feel that no serious harm is done by working with the linear specification (11.6).

The EOp approach is subject to the criticism that it would reduce output by an unacceptable extent. To examine this possibility, I calculated the average (national) wage under two scenarios when $R = \$600$: first, when the educational resource is distributed equally to all students (the conventional interpretation of what equality of opportunity requires), and second, when it is distributed according to the first row of Table 11.2. The average wage (of men aged 30) at educational expenditures x^1 and x^2 is, by definition:

$$p^1 \int \exp[v^1(\pi, x^1)]d\pi + p^2 \int \exp[v^2(\pi, x^2)]d\pi.$$

I found that the average wage falls only 1.4 percent in moving from equal expenditure ($600 per student) to the equal-opportunity expenditure. (This assumes that the age distribution of black and white workers is the same. If white workers tend to be on average older, then the loss of wage income would be greater than indicated, because wages increase with age.) This would seem to be an acceptable price in lost output for equalizing opportunities for earning capacity across races.

The analysis of this section leaves open the question of how type-differentiated educational expenditures should be implemented. This is, in large part, a political problem. Of course, one must imagine that, if a society has gotten to the point that it is willing to implement the kind of EOp policy here advocated, the political problem of how to do so may have largely been solved.

I would propose implementing the differential educational investments here advocated not by issuing vouchers—which would probably lead to criticism from both blacks and whites—but by funding schools in accordance with the distribution of student types within the school. Thus if $R = \$600$, a school which was one-half white and one-half black would receive a per capita student budget of about $1,400 (the appropriate weighted average of $254 and $2,557). Presumably the school would spend its budget in a more or less egalitarian manner within its walls. Were student migration allowed, this approach might well tend to integrate schools, as advantaged white students moved into highly resourced inner-city schools.

To sum up, when we partition the population of U.S. males into just two types, black and white, the EOp policy that uses educational expenditures as the instrument to equalize opportunity for future earning capacity requires vastly larger expenditures on black students than on white students. This is an instance of a surprising statistical fact being double-edged. The statistical fact is that the elasticity of future earnings with respect to educational expenditures appears to be very small, which has been used by conservative observers to argue against further increases of national spending on schools. The second edge of this fact is that, under an EOp policy, vastly larger amounts should thereby be expended on disadvantaged students. In other words, were it to turn out, upon further statistical analysis, that educational spending indeed has a larger impact on future earnings than is now believed, then the differential in the EOp spending between types would diminish, for transferring funds from white students to black students would more quickly reduce the future earnings of the former and increase those of the latter. The other interesting result is that "efficiency," as measured by the total wage bill, would suffer very little under the EOp policy.

§ 12

The Scope and Extent of Equal Opportunity

Should the equal-opportunity principle be applied to admit a certain number of short players, who try very hard, to professional basketball teams? Being short is, after all, a characteristic beyond one's control, and might well be considered a circumstance, were EOp to be applied to basketball recruiting. Should individuals who fail the medical boards in surgery nevertheless be licensed as surgeons if they tried hard, but came from disadvantaged backgrounds? The equal-opportunity principle, if applied, would answer both questions affirmatively. But I would not advocate applying the principle in these cases. What, then, is the scope of the equal-opportunity principle?

It is important to distinguish between two conceptions of equal opportunity: the first being the one I have been elaborating in this book, and the second being the view, widely held, that equal opportunity is part of what is needed to implement a meritocracy. In the second view, individuals should be recruited to positions in society according to their merits, in the sense of J. R. Lucas—that is, according to the attributes they have that are relevant to performing the tasks of the position in question. "Equal opportunity" is a nondiscrimination policy, in this view, which is meant to guarantee that no one with merit is excluded from the pool of candidates because of attributes he has that are irrelevant to the performance required of the position holder. According to this view, effort per se expended by a candidate for the position is irrelevant. Of course, effort expended may well be instrumental for the development of attributes that are necessary for the position, but only the level and quality of those attributes finally matter, not the effort expended. In section 1, I called this second conception of equal opportunity the *nondiscrimination principle*—it might alternatively be called the merit principle—and I shall continue to identify

84

the principle I have been expounding (leveling the playing field) as the *EOp principle*.

The EOp principle counts as an objective only the advantage accruing to the individuals competing for resources (education, health, income); the nondiscrimination or merit principle is concerned not only with the advantage levels of those competitors but also with the welfare of consumers of the product those individuals will produce. Thus basketball players produce a game consumed by spectators, and surgeons produce appendectomies consumed by patients. If we apply the EOp principle to the licensing of surgeons, then we are, in a sense, assigning primary weight to the fulfillment of aspirations of would-be surgeons; if we apply the nondiscrimination principle, we are assigning primary weight to the fulfillment of the lives of patients. In general, of course, one must be concerned with the welfare or advantage accruing to both those who aspire to positions and those whom they serve. It is by limiting the scope and extent of EOp policies that one addresses the welfare of those who are served.

Before proceeding, I must remark that I do not think we can definitively decide the proper scope of the EOp principle without adopting a theory of distributive justice for the community in question. Until now, my purpose has been to describe what equality of opportunity consists in once three decisions have been made: that we shall apply the EOp principle to the situation in question (scope), that the set of circumstances defining type has been determined, and that the amount of resource society shall devote to equalizing opportunities in the situation at hand has been established (extent). On the third of these decisions, a comment is in order. Some situations do not require society to set aside an amount of resource to implement equality of opportunity, because the EOp scheme will be self-financing. This is the case in the health insurance example of section 8 and the unemployment insurance example of section 10. In those examples, the EOp principle is implemented by transfer payments among the class of insured—the rest of society need not set aside any resources. In contrast, in the education examples of sections 9 and 11, we began by supposing that society had set aside a certain amount of resources for educating its children. My claim is that establishing what that amount should be requires a theory of distributive justice for the community as a whole, for society must somehow trade off the consumption of the present generation of adults against the educational level of its children—if, for instance, education is the issue—and hence the degree of fulfillment of the next period's adults.

For example, there might be people who advocate any of the following theories of distributive justice: (1) that, subject to a constraint that opportunities be equalized for children to some specified extent, further allocation of resources be implemented by the market; (2) that, subject to a constraint that opportunities be equalized for the children of each generation to some specified extent, resources be allocated to maximize average utility over the next M generations; and (3) that the minimum level of opportunity for income (or welfare) be maximized over all persons in the next M generations. I could, of course, list other theories of justice. My point is simply that each of a variety of theories might well prescribe equal opportunity in various spheres (health, employment, education), but the scope of equal opportunity and the extent to which opportunities are equalized (which follows from the amount of resource society allocates to that purpose) cannot be deduced without such a theory.

To be precise, the *extent* to which opportunities are equalized is measured by the value of the objective function in (4.2a) at the solution of the program. The more resource society devotes to the problem, the greater will be the size of that objective function at the solution, that is, the value of the EOp program. The reason we must use the value of the EOp objective in measuring the extent of equalization of opportunity is that, in my formulation, we are not concerned with equality as such, but rather with maximizing the opportunities of those who have the least or worst opportunities. Thus it is actually a misnomer to speak of "the extent to which opportunities have been equalized." A more accurate locution would be "the extent to which the equal-opportunity program has been implemented."

My aim in this essay, as I said in the Introduction, has been pluralist, in the sense that I do not wish, here, to argue for a particular theory of distributive justice: I wish, instead, to describe what I think equality of opportunity entails, so that holders of various theories of justice may apply it in the cases where their general theory prescribes it. Given what I have just said, I therefore cannot answer, in a rigorous way, the questions implied by this section's title. Nevertheless, I shall propose a rule of thumb for delineating the spheres of the EOp principle and the nondiscrimination principle that I believe is politically realistic in present-day advanced industrial democracies. This rule of thumb, I think, is consistent with the kinds of trade-off that many, if not all, citizens of many, if not all, such societies would endorse.

I propose that the EOp principle be applied when the advantage in question is the acquisition of an attribute required to compete for a position (a job or career). But I propose that the nondiscrimination principle be applied in the competition for specific positions in society.

Let me elaborate. Having a medical education is an advantage required to compete for certain positions. I advocate applying the EOp principle for admission to medical schools. But becoming a surgeon involves competing for a position: I would apply the nondiscrimination principle in licensing and hiring surgeons. Disadvantaged individuals who try hard but fail the surgery boards would not be licensed, under this rule, nor would a hospital be obligated to hire surgeons who lack the standard attributes.

I would not advocate applying the EOp principle in the recruitment of professional basketball players. I propose, however, that the EOp principle be applied (to short people) in the recruitment of high school basketball players, or even college basketball players: for these teams are, in part, training individuals to compete for positions in society, either as professional basketball players or, more likely, as coaches or other athletic personnel.

There are two generic criticisms that can, I think, be levied against my proposal. The "right-wing" criticism is that my proposal gives too much scope to the EOp principle and not enough to the nondiscrimination principle, and the "left-wing" criticism is that it gives too much scope to the nondiscrimination principle and not enough to the EOp principle. I shall elaborate these criticisms in turn.

What I have called the right-wing criticism is based on the view that application of the EOp principle engenders social inefficiency. It challenges the attempt to distinguish between the formation of general attributes necessary for competing for positions, and competing for positions. If we spend a lot on educating individuals from disadvantaged backgrounds, we will spend correspondingly less on educating highly talented individuals, and consequently we will have fewer people able to take important positions in society which require high levels of talent and training. Applying the EOp principle in medical school admissions will lead to having fewer successful candidates at the surgery boards; if a fixed number of surgeons is needed, it will thus lead to lowering the standards for passing the surgery boards, thereby eventually reducing the general quality of surgery. Indeed, at every level of education or training, the EOp principle would squander social resources, and would lead to the diminution of the pool of well-trained and highly talented individuals which the economy needs to grow and society needs to provide a basket of high-quality goods and services. Society will have met its obligation to equalizing opportunities if it provides equal amounts of educational resources to all individuals through secondary schooling; after that, the competition for positions for further training should be governed by the nondiscrimination principle. Similarly, applying the EOp principle to health insurance is inefficient: health insurance should be supplied by the competitive, private market.

The left-wing critique says that society owes more to disadvantaged individuals than my cut between the two kinds of situation would provide. Consider the case of surgeons. It is so important to have members of certain socially disadvantaged types represented in the surgery profession that we should have different (lower) standards on the surgery boards for such types. Only by having members of these types ascend to the surgery profession will young people from those types begin to form aspirations which will lead them to train themselves for a medical career (the role model effect). Granted, this would reduce the quality of surgery that some patients would receive, but patients should view this reduction as the partial repayment of a debt that society owes its disadvantaged types, recalling that members of those types are, by definition, disadvantaged by virtue of circumstances for which society says they should not be held accountable.

In arguing for the role model effect, the left-wing critic might distinguish between whether the source of an individual's disadvantage is social or inborn. If the source is social, then the role model effect is arguably important; if it is inborn, it is arguably not. For example, that critic could argue that some physicians from socially disadvantaged backgrounds, but who fail the medical boards by the usual standards, should be licensed, because their presence in the profession would lead some children from those backgrounds to aspire to become physicians, with the consequence that by the time *they* have finished medical school, they will pass the boards with no preferential treatment. So the diminution of the quality of surgery engendered by applying the EOp principle would be temporary. In contrast, that critic could not so easily argue that those with low natural intelligence should be preferentially treated at the medical boards, because children of low natural intelligence will never be able to pass the boards by the usual standards. Thus the social/inborn distinction is relevant for the possibility of eventually successful remediation. There are cases, however, where this distinction does not apply for the left-wing critic, who, I am envisioning, would also argue that a mentally handicapped person should be hired in some relatively unskilled job, assuming she is a hard worker, even if she produces a substandard product or service.[22] (This is an application of the EOp principle to the competition for a position.) The right-wing critic would argue against such hiring on grounds of social inefficiency.

As I said, I cannot adjudicate among the three positions (the one I've proposed, the more right-wing, and the more left-wing) without employing an explicit theory of distributive justice for the community in question. But I do not think there is a fundamental issue of rights—which might say, for example, that patients are entitled to the level of proficiency in surgery that the market can supply.

I said that my proposal for the scope of the EOp principle is intended as consistent with what I think a broad section of citizens in many advanced industrial democracies would advocate. Specifically, I think that their judgment would be, first, that the social cost of filling positions with relatively incompetent individuals is greater than the benefit accruing to those individuals from holding those positions, and second, that the benefits to disadvantaged individuals from education and training, and the eventual social benefits from education and training of the disadvantaged, are greater than the immediate social costs of forgone opportunities incurred by applying the EOp principle in such situations. I should emphasize that I am not presupposing that society uses a utilitarian calculus to deduce these social costs and benefits, although it may. Thus I justify the cut not on the basis of individual rights, but by reference to some kind of social welfare function (with which benefits and costs can be computed).

My basis for this evaluation of the views of these citizenries is in part the American experience with affirmative action policy—to be precise, with one specific feature of that experience. Affirmative action policy is under attack

---

22. There are further possibly relevant distinctions, such as between a handicapped worker who produces a standard product, but more slowly than a normal worker, and a handicapped worker who produces a substandard product. If, in the first case, the handicapped worker is paid a commensurately lower wage, there is no social inefficiency. If she is paid a normal wage, through society's subsidizing the private employer, there is a social inefficiency, at least in the narrow sense. If the handicapped worker provides a substandard product and is paid a standard wage, there is also a social inefficiency. Nevertheless, society may prefer the first kind of inefficiency to the second kind, perhaps because, in the first kind, the social cost is relatively anonymous (all consumers contribute a small amount to the subsidy) while in the second case the cost is incident on a small subset of consumers.

in the United States, both in its application in the competition for jobs and in admissions to universities and programs of higher education. There is, however, an important difference in the nature of the attack in these two applications. With regard to the competition for positions, the attack maintains that the most competent candidate should win the job competition, but with regard to university admissions, it maintains that race is not a good measure of disadvantage. Even Ward Connerly, the University of California Regent who spearheaded the successful campaign to end affirmative action admissions policies in the University of California system, says that he supports preferential admissions for students of low socioeconomic status.[23] Thus the attack on the equal-opportunity policy in university admissions focuses not on the application of the principle, but on the delineation of the set of circumstances.

In contrast, the critique of affirmative action in job competitions focuses on the principle itself, arguing, in the language used here, that the nondiscrimination principle is the right one to apply. It is clear that these two criticisms of affirmative action policy are very different: insofar as education and training are concerned, the principle of level the playing field is not called into question, whereas with respect to filling jobs, it is.

To recapitulate, I believe that neither the scope nor the extent of the application of the EOp policy is deducible without a theory of distributive justice for the community. If the theory of justice entails maximizing a social welfare function, as many such theories do, then the net benefits of applying the EOp principle, with various scopes and to various extents, can be calculated. Whatever trade-offs between the welfare or advantage levels of individuals one's theory of distributive justice endorses must ultimately dictate the scope and extent of EOp.

---

23. Connerly said, "UC should use economic status and other genuine hardships when making special admissions, not race." *Sacramento Bee,* May 20, 1995, p. B1.

§ 13

To What Extent Should We Equalize Opportunities?

This section elaborates upon an issue raised in the last section. Take, for the sake of concreteness, the equalization of opportunity for future earning capacity among a society's children, where the resource is educational finance and the instrument with which opportunities are to be equalized is the educational system. There is a set of types, a partition of the society's children into elements each of which contains all the children with a given set of circumstances. The goal is to allocate the educational resource among types in such a way that the distributions of future earning capacity, within the types, are as close as possible to being the same. Naturally, there is some latitude in how we choose to measure closeness of distributions: I have proposed a particular formula in section 4, a kind of maximin operator over distributions.

The question of the extent to which we equalize the opportunities under consideration subdivides into two further questions: (1) how much finance should society set aside for education, and (2) given that budget, how radical should the compensatory spending on disadvantaged types be. I now concentrate on this second question. To equalize opportunities as fully as possible, given the total educational budget, may require spending a much higher amount of that budget, per capita, on children of disadvantaged types. The cost of that policy is that the average level of skill produced in the entire cohort of children—where skill is the output of education—will be lower than if more had been spent on children from more advantaged types. Consequently the goods and services which members of this cohort produce when they, as adults, join the labor force will be fewer and/or of lesser quality than would have been produced by them had the compensatory program been less radical. Thus "society" may pay for its equal-opportunity policy by, in the end, consuming a bundle of goods and services which is inferior, in aggregate, to what it would have otherwise consumed.[24]

To recapitulate an example described earlier, imagine that we implement a policy of equal opportunity in medical school admissions. In particular, we admit to medical schools a certain number of students from disadvantaged backgrounds who don't pass the usual admissions test but who are at the top of their type with respect to that test. Suppose, further, that society decides that board certification for surgeons is not within the scope of equal opportunity, which is to say that no allowance is made for type in judging whether a candidate passes the surgery board examinations.

Nevertheless, if the society needs a fixed number of surgeons, and if there was an equal-opportunity policy at the stage of medical school admissions, then eventually the standards for passing the surgery boards may have to be lowered, to certify the required number of surgeons. It will follow (assuming the surgery boards test the required competence accurately) that the average quality of surgery will fall. Consumers pay later for the equal-opportunity policy incident at the point of medical school admissions. Assuming that society has determined that medical school admissions shall incorporate an equal-opportunity element, to what extent should the policy be followed?

Answering this question requires, as I said earlier, a theory of distributive justice for the entire community. Equal opportunity might well enter differently into a utilitarian's and a resource egalitarian's theory. But the problem may be more subtle still.

I shall now design a model which illustrates these points. In the model I shall circumscribe the question exactly as indicated above: both the scope of equal opportunity policy and the amount of resource to be allocated to its implementation have been determined; only the distribution of the resource among types is in question.

To be specific, this society produces and consumes two goods, called x and y. Society's children acquire skill before they enter the labor force, by the application of a resource, to which they apply effort differentially. There are two types, A(dvantaged), and D(isadvantaged). Members of D require more educational resource to reach the same level of skill as members of A, holding effort constant. Both goods are produced by a linear production function whose sole input is labor. The x good is of homogeneous quality

---

24. I place society in quotes because some members of society will gain and others will lose.

and its quality is independent of the skill levels of the labor that produces it. But the y good's quality depends intimately on the skill of the labor that produces it. Wages in the y industry are higher than in the x industry.

Equal-opportunity policy shall be applied only in the educational process. At the point at which labor is hired, one's type is irrelevant: all that matters is one's skill. Once skills have been realized in people and the labor market opens, we have a market economy where employment is meritorious and nondiscriminatory.[25] Recall that this is the procedure I recommended in section 12.

Consumers derive utility from the amount of both goods and the quality of the y good they consume. To the extent that we engage in an equal-opportunity educational policy, which means we spend proportionally more on D children than on A children in school, the distribution of skills in society will suffer and the quality of the y good eventually produced will decrease, thus decreasing the welfare that consumers, in aggregate, derive from the y good. Our task is to study that trade-off.

Now to specifics. There is a continuum of children; fraction α belong to type A, fraction δ to type D, where $\alpha + \delta = 1$. Production functions of the x good and y good are given by the linear functions

(13.1) $x = L, \qquad y = 2L,$

where L is the amount of labor employed. Further, if the average skill of those employed in the production of a batch of the y good is e, then the quality of that batch is given by

(13.2) $\sigma = qe,$

where q is a positive constant. It is assumed that the firm can produce batches of the y good of different qualities.

As an adult, an individual can consume any (non-negative) amount of the x good. She can consume either zero or one unit of the y good, and must choose the quality of the y good (that is, she can only consume one quality). Her utility function is

(13.3) $u(x, \sigma) = x + v(\sigma).$

---

25. Meritorious means positions are assigned on the basis of skill, not on the basis of type or effort, as I have previously said.

We stipulate that

> (i) v is increasing and concave, and
> (ii) $v(0) = 0$.

By convention, the individual's utility from the y good is $v(0)$ if she consumes zero units and $v(\sigma)$ if she consumes one unit of quality σ.

An amount $\bar{x}$ per capita of the educational resource has been allocated to this generation of children. The policy variable is its distribution between types. If x_0 per capita is allocated to the education of D children, then x_1 per capita is allocated to the education of A children, where

$$(13.4) \qquad x_1 = \frac{\bar{x} - \delta x_0}{\alpha}.$$

Within each type the educational resource is equally distributed.

The distribution of skill among the D type will be a function of x_0: we denote the probability measure that describes it $F_D(\cdot, x_0)$, whose support is the non-negative reals, $\Re_+$. Different individuals in a type realize different skill levels by virtue of applying different levels of effort. The distribution of skills in the A type is denoted $F_A(\cdot, x_1)$.

We assume that

> (iii) $F_J(\cdot, x')$ FOSD $F_J(\cdot, x)$ for $x' > x$, for $J = A, D$.
> (iv) $F_A(\cdot, x')$ FOSD $F_D(\cdot, x)$ for all $x > 0$.

(FOSD stands for "first order stochastically dominates.") This means that skills within type increase with educational spending, and the A type is more effective at converting the educational resource into skill than the D type.

We now define an equilibrium of the market economy, *given* an aggregate distribution of skill, F, of the labor force. We think of $F = \alpha F_A + \delta F_D$, but that decomposition is irrelevant for the definition of equilibrium.

An equilibrium is

> (1) an allocation of all the workers of a given skill level to either the x industry or the y industry,
> (2) a non-negative price function $p(\sigma)$ for the y good, of various qualities σ, such that $p(0) = 0$,

(3) a non-decreasing wage function $w(e)$, for workers of various skill levels e, and

(4) a consumption $x(e)$ and $\sigma(e)$ for the workers of skill level e, with the properties that follow.

We let the price of the x good be one (the numéraire). Let $E_x(E_y)$ be the set of skill levels employed in the x (respectively, y) industry. Then

(i) there is a skill level e^* such that
$$E_y = \{e > e^*\}, \quad E_x = \{e \le e^*\};$$

(ii) (a) for all e, $p(qe) = \frac{1}{2}w(e)$, and
(b) for $e \le e^*$, $w(e) = 1$;

(iii) For all e, $(x(e), \sigma(e))$ solves
$$\max x + v(\sigma)$$
$$\text{s.t. } x + p(\sigma) = w(e);$$

(iv) $\displaystyle\int_{E_x} dF(e) = \int x(e)\, dF(e);$

(v) $\displaystyle\int \Delta(e)\, dF(e) = 2 \int_{E_y} dF(e),$

where $\Delta(e) = \begin{cases} 0 & \text{if } \sigma(e) = 0 \\ 1 & \text{if } \sigma(e) > 0; \end{cases}$

(vi) $\displaystyle \int \sigma(e)\, dF(e) \Big/ \int \Delta(e)\, dF(e) = q \int_{E_y} e\, dF(e) \Big/ \int_{E_y} dF(e).$

Condition (i) states that the x industry hires precisely those workers whose skill levels are less than e^*. Condition (ii) (b) says that the profit-maximizing firm that produces the x good will produce any amount of it, since profits are always zero; condition (ii) (a) says that the y firm maximizes profits by hiring any collection of workers: its profits are always zero. Condition (iii) states that all individuals maximize utility in their consumption choice. Condition (iv) says the demand for labor in the x industry is precisely met by the labor supply E_x. Condition (v) says the demand for labor in the y industry is precisely met by labor supply E_y. Condition (vi) says that the qualities of the y good demanded by consumers are precisely supplied by the y industry. Finally, note that each worker is choosing optimally the industry in which to work. We need only note that no worker in the y industry would like to shift to the x industry, because $w(e)$ is a nondecreasing function. (Thus we assume that a worker can always reduce his skill level but can never increase it.)

I next compute an equilibrium for this economy; I shall not be concerned with whether the equilibrium is unique. It is given by the following.

(a) $e^* = e_M$, where e_M is the median of F;

(b) there is a pair of positive numbers (p, σ^*) solving the following two equations:

$$v'(\sigma^*) = p,$$

$$p \cdot \int_{\sigma^*/2q}^{\infty} (2qe - \sigma^*) \, dF(e) = \tfrac{1}{2};$$

(c) define $w = 2pq$, and define $w(e)$ by

$$w(e) = \begin{cases} we & \text{for } e > e^* \\ 1 & \text{for } e \le e^*; \end{cases}$$

and define $p(\sigma)$ by

$$p(\sigma) = \begin{cases} \tfrac{1}{2} w(\sigma/q) & \text{for } \sigma > qe^* \\[2mm] \tfrac{1}{2} & \text{for } \sigma \le qe^*; \end{cases}$$

(d) for $e \ge \frac{\sigma^*}{2q}$,

$$\sigma(e) = \sigma^*, \quad \text{and} \quad x(e) = we - p\sigma^*;$$

for $e_M < e \le \frac{\sigma^*}{2q}$,

$$\sigma(e) = 2qe, \quad \text{and} \quad x(e) = 0;$$

for $e \le e_M$,

$$x(e) = 0, \quad \text{and} \quad \sigma(e) = \tfrac{1}{p}.$$

In addition, we require that the following conditions hold:

(C1) $\frac{1}{p} < \sigma^*$,

(C2) $\frac{1}{2} + v(qe^*) < v(\frac{1}{p})$,

(C3) $v(\frac{1}{p}) > 1$, and

(C4) $we^* \geq 1$.

Assume we have values $\{e^*, w, p, \sigma^*\}$ satisfying (C1)–(C4) and functions $\sigma(e), x(e), p(\sigma), w(e)$ as specified in (a)–(d). We must check that these constitute an equilibrium. Readers who wish to skip the proof should proceed to the end-of-proof mark.

We first verify profit maximization. The x firm makes zero profits as long as it hires workers for whom $e \leq e^*$, for their wages are one and the price of output is one (and $x = L$). It makes negative profits if it hires any other workers. Thus assigning the set of workers E_x to the x firm is a profit-maximizing allocation. The y firm can hire any collection of workers and make zero profits: this follows from the wage and price functions specified in (c). [Note that if the firm hires one worker of skill level $e > e^*$, that worker produces two units of the y good of quality qe. Since $p(qe) = w(e)/2$, the firm makes zero profit on the transaction. A similar argument holds for $e < e^*$.]

We next verify that, at the allocation given in (d), every consumer is maximizing utility. First, note that, from (c), for $\sigma > qe^*$, we have $p(\sigma) = p\sigma$.

Consumer maximization for a consumer with income I can be written

$$\max I - p(\sigma) + v(\sigma)$$
$$\text{s.t. } I - p(\sigma) \geq 0.$$

Note that, by definition of p and σ^*, $v(\sigma) - p\sigma$ is increasing in the interval $[0, \sigma^*)$.

We partition the domain of individuals into three regions, based on skill, and verify the claimed consumptions for each in turn. In the first, $e \leq e^*$. The income of these workers is one; hence their maximization program is

$$\max v(\sigma) - p(\sigma)$$
$$\text{s.t. } p(\sigma) \leq 1.$$

Suppose, first, that these agents consume one unit of the y good (that is, $\sigma > 0$). There are two possibilities for the solution: either

$$\sigma = qe^* \quad \text{and} \quad x = \tfrac{1}{2},$$

in which case utility is $\tfrac{1}{2} + v(qe^*)$, or

$$\sigma = \tfrac{1}{p} \quad \text{and} \quad x = 0,$$

in which case utility is $v(\tfrac{1}{p})$. The first subcase is the solution of the program in the interval $\sigma \leq qe^*$, while the second subcase is the solution of the consumer's program restricted to the interval $\sigma > qe^*$. [To see this, note that $\sigma^* > \tfrac{1}{p}$, by (C1), and use the fact that $v(\sigma) - p\sigma$ is increasing in the interval $[0, \sigma^*)$.]

Hence the consumer with income one, if she chooses to consume one unit of the y good, chooses $\sigma = \tfrac{1}{p}$ and $x = 0$ as long as

(13.5) $\qquad \tfrac{1}{2} + v(qe^*) < v\left(\tfrac{1}{p}\right),$

which holds by (C2). Finally, because $v(\tfrac{1}{p}) > 1$, by (C3) the consumer indeed does choose to consume one unit, rather than zero units, of the y good.

Second, consider the case where e is in the interval $(e^*, \tfrac{\sigma^*}{2q})$. Suppose this consumer consumes one unit of the y good. Then this consumer will choose either

$$\sigma = qe^* \quad \text{and} \quad x = w(e) - \tfrac{1}{2},$$

in which case utility is $w(e) - \tfrac{1}{2} + v(qe^*)$, or she will choose

$$\sigma = \tfrac{we}{p} \quad \text{and} \quad x = 0,$$

in which case utility is $v(\tfrac{we}{p})$. (Again, the second subcase is the maximization of the consumer's utility in the interval $\sigma > qe^*$. To see this, use the fact that $\tfrac{we}{p} < \sigma^*$, which follows from the assumption that $e < \tfrac{\sigma^*}{2q}$ in this *case*.)

Thus this consumer, if she consumes the y good, chooses $\sigma = \tfrac{we}{p} = 2qe$ and $x = 0$, as long as

(13.6) $\qquad w(e) - \tfrac{1}{2} + v(qe^*) < v\left(\tfrac{we}{p}\right).$

To verify (13.6), note that both (13.5) and (13.6) are of the form

(13.7) $v\left(\frac{I}{p}\right) - I > v(qe^*) - \frac{1}{2},$

where I is the agent's income. Now note that the left-hand side of (13.7) is an increasing function of I, for I in the interval $[0, p\sigma^*]$. The largest income in this *case* is $w\sigma^*/2q$, which equals $p\sigma^*$. Hence (13.6) holds, since (13.5) holds, by this monotonicity argument.

Finally, this consumer indeed does choose to consume one unit of the y good, because $v(\frac{I}{p}) - I > v(\frac{1}{p}) - 1 > 0$, again invoking monotonicity of the left-hand side of (13.7).

The third case to consider is $e \geq \frac{\sigma^*}{2q}$. In like manner, if this consumer consumes one unit of the y good, he chooses either

$$\sigma = qe^* \quad \text{and} \quad x = we - \frac{1}{2},$$

in which case utility is $we - \frac{1}{2} + v(qe^*)$, or

$$\sigma = \sigma^* \quad \text{and} \quad x = we - p\sigma^*,$$

in which case utility is $we - p\sigma^* + v(\sigma^*)$. This consumer chooses

$$\sigma = \sigma^* \quad \text{and} \quad x = we - p\sigma^*$$

as long as

(13.8) $-\frac{1}{2} + v(qe^*) < v(\sigma^*) - p\sigma^*.$

But inequality (13.8) is of the form (13.7), where $I - p\sigma^*$, and hence follows by the same monotonicity argument. In like manner, this consumer indeed does choose to consume one unit of the y good.

We have verified that consumer maximization, at the prices given by (c), is given by the allocation specified in (d).

Finally, we study market clearing. From the above analysis, we see that the total demand for the x good comes from those consumers with $e \geq \sigma^*/2q$. That demand, in per capita terms, is $\int_{\sigma^*/2q}^{\infty}(we - p\sigma^*)\, dF(e) = p \int_{\sigma^*/2q}^{\infty}(2qe - \sigma^*)\, dF(e)$. Hence this is also the total demand for labor, in per capita terms, in the x industry (since $x = L$). Now the total demand for labor in the y industry, in per capita terms, is $1/2$, since as we have shown, each citizen demands one unit of the y good (and $y = 2L$). It therefore follows that at equilibrium:

$$p \int_{\sigma^*/2q}^{\infty} (2qe - \sigma^*) \, dF(e) = \tfrac{1}{2},$$

as part (b) says.

Since one-half the population is employed in each industry, we assign the less-skilled part to the x industry: this is precisely what (a) accomplishes. Next we must show that the workers in the y industry are just capable of producing the quality of y goods demanded (condition (vi)). The average quality demand of the y good is

(13.9)
$$\int_0^{e_M} \tfrac{1}{p} dF(e) + \int_{e_M}^{\sigma^*/2q} (2qe) \, dF(e) + \int_{\sigma^*/2q}^{\infty} \sigma^* dF(e)$$

$$= \tfrac{1}{2p} + 2q \int_{e_M}^{\sigma^*/2q} e \, dF(e) + \sigma^* \left(1 - F\left(\tfrac{\sigma^*}{2q} \right) \right).$$

The average quality of the y good supplied is

(13.10) $$q \int_{e_M}^{\infty} \frac{e \, dF(e)}{\tfrac{1}{2}} = 2q \int_{e_M}^{\infty} e \, dF(e).$$

Hence we must verify that the expressions in (13.9) and (13.10) are equal. Using (b), we can substitute for the term $1/2p$ in (13.9), and write

$$\int_{\sigma^*/2q}^{\infty} (2qe - \sigma^*) \, dF(e) + \int_{e_M}^{\sigma^*/2q} 2qe \, dF(e)$$

$$+ \int_{\sigma^*/2q}^{\infty} \sigma^* \, dF(e) = 2q \int_{e_M}^{\infty} e \, dF(e),$$

an identity, as required.

This verifies that the proposed allocation and prices constitute an equilibrium. ∎

The next step is to simulate the model. I shall specify

$$q = \tfrac{1}{2}, \quad \text{and} \quad v(\sigma) = 2a\sigma^{1/2}.$$

I assume that the measures $F_D(\cdot, x)$ and $F_A(\cdot, x)$ are exponential, given by the densities

$$f_A(e; x_1) = \lambda_A \exp(-\lambda_A e),$$
$$f_D(e; x_0) = \lambda_D \exp(-\lambda_D e),$$

where

(13.11) $\frac{1}{\lambda_A} = m_1 x_1, \qquad \frac{1}{\lambda_D} = m_0 x_0, \qquad m_1 > m_0.$

Since $1/\lambda$ is the mean of the exponential distribution, this says that mean skill level of a type is a linear function of the amount spent on the education of its members. Further, recall that if $\bar{x}$ is the social per capita allotment to education, and x_0 per capita is allocated to the D type, then x_1 per capita is allocated to the A type, where x_1 is given by (13.4).

If λ_A and λ_D characterize the skill distributions among the two types, then the skill distribution in society is given by the probability measure

$$F(\cdot) = \alpha F_A(\cdot) + \delta F_D(\cdot).$$

We may then compute the equilibrium equations, given in part (c) of the specification of the equilibrium, as

$$p = v'(\sigma^*)$$

(13.12) $p \left\{ e^{-\lambda_A \sigma^*} \frac{\alpha}{\lambda_A} + \frac{\delta}{\lambda_D} e^{-\lambda_D \sigma^*} \right\} = \frac{1}{2},$

where the median e_M is given by

(13.13) $\alpha e^{-\lambda_A e_M} + \delta e^{-\lambda_D e_M} = \frac{1}{2}.$

(I apologize for the potential confusion between e, denoting skill, and the natural constant, e.) With a choice of parameters $(a, \alpha, \delta, \bar{x}, m_0, m_1)$ we can compute the equilibria at various values of x_0.

I report some results for $a = 3$, $\alpha = 0.75$, $\delta = 0.25$, $\bar{x} = 0.20$, $m_0 = 1$, $m_1 = 2$. Full equality of opportunity occurs when the educational resource is distributed so that

(13.14) $m_0 x_0 = m_1 x_1,$

Table 13.1   Equilibrium values at various distributions of the educational resource

x_0	e_M	σ^*	σ_{lo}	p	wel$_D$	wel$_A$	avewel
0.20	0.231	0.427	0.218	4.589	3.149	3.944	3.746
0.22	0.231	0.415	0.215	4.655	3.21	3.888	3.718
0.24	0.231	0.404	0.212	4.719	3.276	3.83	3.691
0.26	0.229	0.394	0.209	4.779	3.349	3.771	3.666
0.28	0.228	0.385	0.207	4.836	3.426	3.712	3.641
0.30	0.225	0.376	0.204	4.89	3.507	3.653	3.617
0.32	0.222	0.368	0.202	4.942	3.593	3.593	3.593

for at that point, the distribution of skills is identical for the two types. For these parameters, (13.14) occurs at $x_0 = 0.32$, $x_1 = 0.16$. In Table 13.1, I report what happens to various equilibrium values as we alter x_0 from 0.20 to 0.32. When $x_0 = x_1 = .20$, we devote the same amount of educational resource to all children.

Each row of Table 13.1 reports characteristics of the equilibrium of the model, computed for that distribution, F, of skills, engendered by distributing the educational resource according to the value determined by the first element in the row. Conditions (C1)–(C4) hold for every row, and so, indeed, these values are genuine equilibria. In Table 13.1, σ_{lo} is the quality of the y good consumed by workers in the x industry; σ^* is the quality of the y good consumed by the cohort of sufficiently skilled individuals. I report the price, p, per unit quality of the y good, as well.

We see that the average welfare of the D type (wel$_D$) increases and that the average welfare of the A type falls, as we proceed from $x_0 = x_1 = .20$ to full equality of opportunity, at $x_0 = 0.32$, $x_1 = .16$. The trade-off between equalizing opportunities and the quality of the consumption good is evident in the declining value of σ^* and σ_{lo}. As opportunities become equalized, the range of qualities of the y good produced decreases unambiguously. Indeed, not only does the cohort of highly skilled individuals consume lower qualities of the y good as opportunities are equalized, but so does the bottom half of the skill distribution, for they are employed in the x industry, and consume the quality σ_{lo}. Nevertheless, on average, disadvantaged individuals fare better as opportunities are equalized, because, although the price of quality is rising, an increasing fraction of the disadvantaged type are hired in the y industry, and thus earn higher wages. Note that the greatest lower bound of wages paid in the y industry is pe_M, which is higher than the wage of 1 paid in the x industry.

I now observe that the last row of Table 13.1 represents, in fact, the solution of the EOp objective (4.2a) for the problem at hand, where we restrict policies to assign a fixed per capita amount of resource to each type. This is so because, for values x_0 in the interval $[.20, .32]$, $\min[V^D(\pi; x_0), V^A(\pi; x_1)] = V^D(\pi; x_0)$, where $V^D(\pi; x_0)$ is the utility of the individual at centile π of the effort distribution of type D, when x_0 has been invested in D's education, at equilibrium. (See below for the exact definition of V^D and V^A.) Therefore, the solution of (4.2a) is the solution of

$$\max_{x_0} \int_0^1 V^D(\pi; x_0)\, d\pi$$
$$0 \le x_0 \le .32.$$

But this integral is just average utility of the D type, which is maximized at $x_0 = .32$ (see the last row of the "wel$_D$" column of Table 13.1).

We see, from Table 13.1, how the extent to which one advocates equal opportunity depends upon one's theory of distributive justice. The last column reports average welfare in society. Thus a utilitarian, forced to choose among the allocations in the table, would choose $x_0 = x_1 = 0.20$. (She might prefer allocating even more of the educational resource to the A type, unless her utilitarianism were constrained by some condition of "formal" equal educational opportunity.) An opportunity egalitarian who solves the program (4.2a) would advocate $x_0 = 0.32$, as the previous paragraph shows.

One response to the "equality-efficiency trade-off" evident in Table 13.1 would be to spend the same amount of educational resource on all children, but to transfer income from the advantaged to the disadvantaged through income taxation. That move is, however, not ethically costless, for three reasons. First, income taxation brings with it its own inefficiencies; second, in reality, though not in this model, individuals derive self-esteem from working at more skilled jobs (the y industry), which cannot be entirely replaced with income transfers; and third, income taxes transfer income not only from the advantaged to the disadvantaged type but from the high-effort to the low-effort individuals within type, and that is not clearly desirable from an equal-opportunity view.[26] For these reasons, income taxation is not a panacea, although doubtless one would be foolish to reject using it completely.

By construction, in the example of the simulation, opportunities for future welfare are unambiguously equalized at $x_0 = .32$ and $x_1 = .16$. One initially troublesome aspect of that equalization is that the quality of the y good produced by society is reduced from the "equal resource" allocation, where $x_0 = 0.20$. To someone who is concerned about opportunities for welfare, this reduction is irrelevant: it would be commodity fetishist, or perfectionist, to bemoan changes in the nature of goods per se, apart from their effects on human welfare. As we move down the rows of Table 13.1, more members of the disadvantaged type are becoming surgeons, and are consequently better off, by virtue of the relatively high wages in surgery, although society receives a lower quality of surgery than before, on average.

It does behoove us, however, to examine more precisely what happens to the welfare of *individuals* as we move from the first to the last row of Table 13.1. To do so, we need to be able to locate the path of each individual in that transition. Let us postulate, reasonably, that a given member of either type retains her same relative place in the distribution of effort (and therefore of skill) of her type as the resource endowment devoted to her type's education changes. Then we can identify each individual with a number π between 0 and 1, which is her centile in the skill distribution of her type.

Let $e_D(\pi, x_0)$ be the skill level achieved by the individual at the πth centile of the skill distribution of the D type when the educational investment in that type is x_0 per capita. By definition,

$$(13.15a) \quad \pi = F_D(e_D(\pi, x_0); x_0),$$

where $F_D(\cdot; x_0)$ is the cumulative distribution function of skill in the D type when the educational investment is x_0. In like manner, we can define $e_A(\pi, x_1)$ for the A type by

$$(13.15b) \quad \pi = F_A(e_A(\pi, x_1); x_1).$$

---

26. The equal-opportunity view says that those of a given type who expend more effort should fare better than those who expend less, but it does not tell us how much better. Is the market allocation of incomes, given that opportunities have been equalized, too extreme?

Recalling that we are working with the exponential distributions defined earlier, we may solve (13.15a and b) for $e_D(\pi, x_0)$ and $e_A(\pi, x_1)$;

$$e_D(\pi, x_0) = -m_0 x_0 \log(1 - \pi),$$

and $$e_A(\pi, x_1) = -m_1 x_1 \log(1 - \pi).$$

Using the characterization of the equilibrium allocation derived earlier, we can now write the utility of an individual at the πth centile of the D type, when the expenditure is x_0, as

$$V^D(\pi; x_0) = \begin{cases} v(1/p), & \text{if } e_D(\pi, x_0) \leq e_M \\ v(e_D(\pi, x_0)), & \text{if } e_M < e_D(\pi, x_0) < \sigma^* \\ v(\sigma^*) + p(e_D(\pi, x_0) - \sigma^*), & \text{if } e_D(\pi, x_0) \geq \sigma^*. \end{cases}$$

A similar formula holds for the indirect utility function $V^A(\pi; x_1)$, which gives the utility of the individual at the πth centile of the A type at the educational expenditure x_1.

In Figure 13.1, I graph the function $V^D(\pi; x_0)$ for the values $x_0 = .20$ and .32 (that is, corresponding to the first and last rows of Table 13.1). The flat segments of the two graphs correspond to the utility of individuals who find employment in the x industry. We note that those who exert effort in the bottom half of the effort distribution in the D type fare worse under the equal-opportunity policy than under the equal-resource ($x_0 = .20$) policy. Figure 13.2 presents the graphs of $V^A(\pi; x_1)$ corresponding to the first and last rows of Table 13.1. We see that all individuals of the A type do worse under the equal-opportunity policy than under the equal-resource policy. In the simulation, since $\alpha = .75$ and $\delta = .25$, this means that 87.5 percent of the population becomes worse off in moving from the equal-resource to the equal-opportunity policy. The only benefactors of the full-opportunity egalitarian policy are the individuals in the more industrious half of the disadvantaged type.

I feel that we may go too far if we implement the full-opportunity egalitarian policy in this economy. Suppose we go less far—suppose, to be concrete, we move only from the first to the second row of Table 13.1. It turns out that in this case, the welfare of everyone in the A type falls, and the welfare of approximately 65 percent of those in the D type falls, because about 65 percent of the D type remains employed in the x industry in the equilibrium

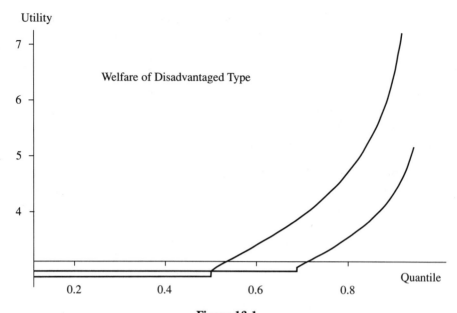

Figure 13.1
Welfare levels of individuals in the D type, equal resources
and equal opportunity

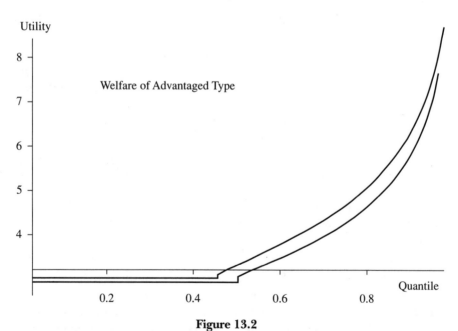

Figure 13.2
Welfare levels of individuals in the A type, equal resources
and equal opportunity

of the second row of Table 13.1. Of course, the changes in welfare are quite small in moving from the first to the second row of Table 13.1, but it is the case that 91 percent of the individuals in society sustain a fall in welfare in this move.

It should not bother us that the welfare levels of members of the A type fall in the policy changes I've described, for those persons are, by supposition, benefiting unjustly by virtue of circumstance. But I do see reason to be bothered by the fall in welfare levels of a substantial fraction of the D type. The important qualitative aspect of the example is that in seeking to equalize opportunities for welfare among the types, the welfare levels of members of the disadvantaged type do not all move in the same direction. This nonmonotonicity is, however, due not to circumstance or luck, but to the peculiarities, so to speak, of the Walrasian allocation mechanism and the exponential distribution.

In conclusion, and to reiterate, the principle of equal opportunity alone may be insufficient to resolve the issue of extent. This section has raised an issue additional to ones discussed in section 12, namely, that implementing equal opportunity may harm a substantial proportion of the members of disadvantaged types whose opportunities the policy was putatively designed to enhance. The fully committed opportunity egalitarian might say that yes, the opportunities of every member of the disadvantaged type *do* improve in the move from the equal-resource to the equal-opportunity educational policy—however, some members do not realize those opportunities by ex-erting sufficient effort. Still, the fact that one-half the population of the type actually fares worse under the opportunity-egalitarian policy is, for me, a problem.

§14

Affirmative Action

We have seen, in sections 9 and 11, one example of affirmative action: implementing equality of opportunity may require spending more educational resources, per capita, on children from disadvantaged types. One popular view, that this policy necessarily entails an inefficient use of educational resources, is incorrect, by virtue of its incorrect identification of the (social) maximandum. If total output were the maximandum, then, indeed, it might be inefficient to spend more resources on less-advantaged children. If, however, the social maximandum is the equality-of-opportunity objective, then such a distribution of the educational resource is not inefficient. In plain words, what may be inefficient from the viewpoint of maximizing GNP may not be inefficient from the viewpoint of equalizing opportunity. This simple point, that a society committed to equality of opportunity will generally have a lower GNP per capita than a society committed to maximizing GNP per capita, is not well understood in the popular discussion.

I will define affirmative action as preferential treatment, in social policy, of some types over others, where types are defined, as in section 2, as classes of persons characterized by particular values of vectors of characteristics for which society deems individuals should not be held accountable. It is instructive to analyze the current popular discussion of affirmative action with this definition in mind.

The first issue is the nature of the justification for affirmative action given in the popular debate. It is sometimes said that affirmative action is justified on grounds of retributive justice, that is, to compensate living persons for the unjust treatment of their ancestors. Even if advocates of affirmative action do not often use this argument, many critics of affirmative action take this argument to be its justification. (Anyone who listens to talk shows on American radio will have often heard critics of affirmative

108

action use it.) This is, I think, a bad argument. (For further elaboration, see Elster 1993.) Whose welfare is being increased by such compensation? Surely not that of the dead ancestors.[27] Now if the welfare of the ancestors enters significantly into the utility function of their living descendant, then one could argue that such preferential treatment (of live descendants) is justified: those descendants, under this premise, have lower welfare than other persons today on account of something beyond their control, namely, the abnormally bad treatment of their ancestors. But I find the premise to be incredible. The direct "consumption" effect on the great-grandchildren of slaves from their great-grandparents' having suffered greatly is probably quite small. (By this I mean the illfare a person feels when thinking about the horrible life of his slave ancestor.)

What may not be small, however, is the influence of a living individual's great-grandparents' having been slaves on the availability of resources, generally construed, to him today. It may be debated whether having had slaves in one's ancestry *does* have a causal relation to one's "resource endowment." But if it does, whether through its direct effect on the wealth of descendants, on the culture of descendants, on the self-esteem of descendants, or on the treatment of descendants by others in society, which may affect their income-earning capacity or self-esteem, it is an admissible dimension of type.

A second issue deserving comment concerns the kind of affirmative action in which members of a "disadvantaged" type are allocated positions in the production process when others, whose productivity would be greater in those positions, are passed over. I have discussed this issue in section 12.

When a relatively incompetent person from a disadvantaged type is awarded a scarce position, it is frequently said that a person more deserving than the member of the disadvantaged type should have gotten it. "More deserving" can mean one of two things: either that (i) the person passed over was from a type that was more disadvantaged than the type from which the winner in the job competition came, or (ii) that the person passed over was more qualified for the job, in the sense of being more productive in that job

---

27. There is a philosophical position, however, that maintains that a dead person's welfare can change by virtue of what occurs after her death. If welfare is the degree to which one's life plan is fulfilled, this is the case, as that degree may not be settled for some time after the person's death. As Zhou Enlai responded when asked about the significance of the French Revolution, "It's too early to tell."

than the one who got it. Only sense (i) of "more deserving" concerns us in this paragraph—sense (ii) shall concern us in the next. If the person passed over was from a more disadvantaged type, then his complaint may be justified on EOp grounds. Indeed, the white working-class backlash against U.S. affirmative action policies may be partially justified on these grounds: the complaint being made, in terms of our categories, is that class background is a more relevant dimension of type than race with respect to a causal link to disadvantage. (This is, of course, an empirical question. It is well known that class data have never been collected in the U.S. Census, in contrast with the United Kingdom, and that, consequently, race is often used as an imperfect proxy for class in the United States. Race-based affirmative action policies may well be an instance of this more general American error.) If desert, so construed, is taken as a criterion for the distribution of scarce positions, then the EOp principle requires allocating positions equally (so far as is possible) to persons of all types at the same percentiles of their "effort" distributions. In particular, a black student (let us say) with SAT scores of 900 may be at the same centile of "effort" as a white student with SAT scores of 1100, if effort is taken to be some measure of students' application in high school, and frequency distributions of effort are calculated by type.

Argument (ii) has two possible interpretations: either (iia) that she who has the greater degree of job-relevant attributes deserves the position on that account alone, or (iib) that she who has the greater degree of job-relevant attributes deserves the position because she will be more productive in it (that is, produce a better product or service for society).

It might be thought that view (iia) follows from what is called, in political philosophy, the thesis of self-ownership, which G. A. Cohen defines as follows: "Each person possesses over himself, as a matter of moral right, all those rights that a slaveholder has over a complete chattel slave as a matter of legal right, and he is entitled, morally speaking, to dispose over himself in the way such a slaveholder is entitled, legally speaking, to dispose over his slave" (Cohen 1995, p. 68). In particular, the thesis of self-ownership says that a person should have private ownership rights over her attributes, and therefore is entitled to sell her services in the market: coercive taxation of such income, for example, constitutes a morally unjustifiable incursion against that property right. I think that the thesis of self-ownership may well be used against affirmative action policies, which favor some types over others, for such policies do abrogate the market. I do not, however, believe that self-ownership shows, as argument (iia) claims, that the owner of an attribute deserves a position: rather, she would be, on self-ownership grounds, entitled to it. Here I refer again to Lucas's distinction: one deserves something because of what one has done, not because of what one has by legal right.

Argument (iib) is more plausible, and as I have said in section 12, whether it is correct depends on the costs and benefits of hiring relatively incompetent individuals in various jobs. I have included, among those costs, the consequences of backlash, which might render the costs (of applying affirmative action) greater than the benefits.

There is a duplicity in the justification of affirmative action policies in the United States that may have contributed significantly to the backlash against the policy. Affirmative action is often described by those advocating it as the nondiscrimination form of equal opportunity: the policy, it is held, requires only that all those who possess the attributes relevant for performing the duties of the position in question be included in the pool of eligible candidates, but that once the pool has been delimited, then the person "most qualified" should be chosen for the job (with tie-breaking done, perhaps, with an eye to past disadvantage).[28] But the policy as implemented is often, if not usually, one of the EOp form: that is, different standards of "competency" are applied to individuals of different types. Indeed, when a federal regulation or statute requires certain "goals" or "timetables," then institutions (firms, universities) must usually apply the EOp version of equal opportunity in order to make any progress according to the stipulated statistical measures: that is, they must hire a certain number of disadvantaged candidates to meet the goal, even if they are relatively incompetent. If arguments were given for the moral correctness of the EOp approach, instead of falsely claiming that only the nondiscrimination approach was being applied, it is possible that backlash would be considerably less than it has been. After all, how can one expect members of the public to accept what they correctly see as (an approximation to) the EOp policy, when they are told that only the nondiscrimination principle is being affirmed?

---

28. An instance of the duplicity is visible in the following. President Clinton insists that affirmative action requires that only the most qualified individual in the eligible pool be hired for the position. But he also asks all federal agencies to examine whether the time has come to terminate their affirmative action policies. Does this mean that he suggests a time will come when agencies should cease hiring only the most qualified? Clearly not— it means just the opposite, that a time will come when preference for those who are *not* the most qualified will not be necessary. But this, of course, directly contradicts his claim that affirmative action policy requires hiring only the most qualified in the pool.

My view, as I've said, is that the EOp policy should be implemented whenever the benefits exceed the costs. (As we saw in section 13, that benefit-cost calculation may be difficult.) This evaluation, however, requires the use of a particular social welfare function. While we cannot hope, in a diverse society, that all citizens will agree to employ the same social welfare function, we can hope that most will agree on some policy of equal opportunity. My compromise proposal, explained in section 12, is intended as a politically realistic one: apply the EOp principle for the acquisition of attributes necessary to compete for careers and jobs, but apply the non-discrimination principle in the recruitment of job holders. The second part of this proposal would, I think, be acceptable to the vast majority of citizens. To win acceptance of the first part would require a principled argument for the EOp view, one avoiding the duplicity that characterizes present practice.

Two more arguments against affirmative action, of the EOp variety, should be mentioned. The first maintains that the policy does not succeed in raising the welfare of the members of the disadvantaged types. Two reasons are frequently given: people do not derive welfare—in particular, self-esteem—from being placed in positions in which they produce less competently than others in those positions, and there is a backlash created by placing such persons in those positions which acts to the detriment of the members of the disadvantaged type, quite generally. The second reason may, of course, be due to society's nonacceptance of EOp as an objective: it may call for more social discussion of the importance of leveling the playing field, rather than for ending the policy. The loss of self-esteem from relative incompetence on the job is itself in part due to backlash, but perhaps only in part. There are surely situations, for example, in which disabled persons enjoy large gains in self-esteem from holding jobs which they perform relatively incompetently, if their presence on the job is warmly supported by more able colleagues. This suggests that no small part of the loss of self-esteem putatively experienced by beneficiaries of affirmative action who are relatively incompetent in their jobs may be due to the impatience of their colleagues.

Finally, some advance the argument that affirmative action may result in perpetuating the disadvantaged status of the less-advantaged or -privileged type, because of its bad incentive properties. The argument is fully spelled out by Loury (1995). Briefly, the idea is that, in order to meet government-imposed hiring quotas, firms may hire unqualified workers of the less-advantaged type; knowing this, workers from the disadvantaged type have less incentive than otherwise to acquire skills. Loury, however, also shows that this deleterious outcome can be prevented by the government's imposing a sequence of quotas, which increase gradually to some desired level, rather than immediately requiring a large increase in the proportion of the disadvantaged type hired. More generally, Loury's example is a special case of the problem discussed in section 5, that preferential treatment of disadvantaged types may reduce the effort expended by those types. In that section, I have explained the general procedure for treating this possibility.

§15

Concluding Remarks

I have taken a micro-oriented approach in this study by asking how social resources should be distributed among a target population to equalize members' opportunities for acquiring a stipulated kind of success or advantage. In contrast, a macro-oriented approach toward equalizing opportunities in respect of health might include outlawing the advertising of cigarettes; in respect of education, it might include extending the school-leaving age by one year (which would de facto increase the years of school attended by disadvantaged types more than advantaged types) or reducing the unemployment rate of high school graduates through fiscal or monetary policy; in respect of unemployment, it might attempt to change the characteristics of jobs in the secondary sector, or reduce the number of such jobs (for instance, by raising the minimum wage).

I do not wish to imply that only the micro approach should be used, or even that it is more effective than the macro approach. I believe, quite the contrary, that often the macro approach may be more effective, at least up to a point. My analysis, rather, should be understood as applying after society has put in place its macro policies which address the alleviation of disadvantage. For, after those policies are in place, inequality of opportunity will remain, and society must face the question of how to allocate various resources among types of citizen in a fair way.

There is also, as the reader will have noticed, a substantial degree of latitude in how, precisely, one applies the EOp algorithm to arrive at an equal-opportunity policy. One must choose a measure of success or advantage, a definition of type, a measure of effort, a set of admissible policies, the specific form of the allocation rules, and finally the method by which resources are ultimately delivered to the individuals in question. (By this last item, I refer, for instance, to the choice of distributing educational resources via

114

vouchers given to students or budgets given to schools, as discussed briefly in section 11.) Some of these choices involve issues of values (how to measure advantage), others concern issues of incentive compatibility and asymmetry of information (can effort be observed? can types be observed?), political issues (the definition of type, the possibility of backlash), or issues of statistical availability (do we have studies enabling us to compute the distributions of effort according to type and allocation rule?). Because I have not provided a complete recipe for solving the various problems these issues raise, my advertisement of this study as providing an algorithm for equalizing opportunities is perhaps misleading.

Moreover, I have concentrated on describing what constitutes equality of opportunity. I have only begun to study the questions of scope and extent: to what kinds of social contest should equality of opportunity apply, and when it should apply, to what extent should we implement it? These are open questions.

References

Arneson, R. 1989. "Equality and equal opportunity for welfare." *Philosophical Studies* 56, 77–93.

——— 1990. "Liberalism, distributive subjectivism, and equal opportunity for welfare." *Philosophy & Public Affairs* 19, 159–194.

Betts, J. 1996. "Is there a link between school inputs and earnings? Fresh scrutiny of an old literature." In G. Burtless, ed., *Does Money Matter? The Effect of School Resources on Student Achievement and Adult Success.* Washington, D.C.: Brookings Institution.

Cohen, G. A. 1989. "On the currency of egalitarian justice." *Ethics* 99, 906–944.

——— 1993. "Equality of what? On welfare, goods, and capabilities." In Martha C. Nussbaum and Amartya Sen, eds., *The Quality of Life.* Oxford: Clarendon Press.

——— 1995. *Self-Ownership, Freedom, and Equality.* Cambridge: Cambridge University Press.

Dworkin, R. 1981a. "What is equality? Part 1: Equality of welfare." *Philosophy & Public Affairs* 10, 185–246.

——— 1981b. "What is equality? Part 2: Equality of resources." *Philosophy & Public Affairs* 10, 283–345.

Elster, J. 1993. "Ethical individualism and presentism." *The Monist* 76, 333–348.

Herrnstein, R. J., and C. Murray. 1994. *The Bell Curve.* New York: Free Press.

Jensen, A. R. 1969. "How much can we boost IQ and scholastic achievement?" *Harvard Educational Review* 39, 1–123.

Loury, G. 1995. "Conceptual problems in the enforcement of anti-discrimination laws." Dept. of Economics, Boston University.

Lucas, J. R. 1995. *Responsibility.* Oxford: Clarendon Press.

Ortega y Gasset, J. 1914. "Meditaciones del Quijote." In *Obras Completas,* vol I. Madrid: Revista de Occiente, 1983.

Roemer, J. 1996. *Theories of Distributive Justice.* Cambridge, Mass.: Harvard University Press.

Scanlon, T. 1986. "Equality of resources and equality of welfare: A forced marriage?" *Ethics* 97, 111–118.

———— 1988. "The significance of choice." In S. McMurrin, ed., *The Tanner Lectures on Human Values,* vol. 8. Salt Lake City: University of Utah Press.

Sen, A. 1985. *Commodities and Capabilities.* Amsterdam: North-Holland.

Index